The Fight for the Family

The Adults Behind Children's Rights

Lynette Burrows

FAMILY EDUCATION TRUST

OXFORD

D0318045

The Fight for the Family

The Adults Behind Children's Rights

© **FAMILY EDUCATION TRUST, 1998**

ISBN 0 906229 14 6

First published January 1998
Revised and reprinted March 1999

published by
FAMILY EDUCATION TRUST
A Company Limited by Guarantee
322 WOODSTOCK ROAD · OXFORD OX2 7NS
Tel: 01865 351 966   *Fax:* 01865 351 967

Printed in England by the Cromwell Press, Trowbridge

About the author

Lynette Burrows was born in London. She graduated at the University of Hull and took a post-graduate degree at London University. She became an Assistant Lecturer in English and Law before marrying. Although a full-time mother of six children, she lectures and broadcasts extensively on social issues. Her book *Good Children* was described as 'so old-fashioned as to be positively radical' and is in the process of being reprinted for the third time.

Acknowledgements

The author would like to thank Melissa Sheldon of Grand Rapids, Michigan, USA for her invaluable help, encouragement and professionalism in researching much of the material for this book; and Stephen Green, author of *The Sexual Dead End,* on whose research Chapter 5 is largely based.

Contents

Foreword

When *The Fight for the Family* was first released to the press in January 1998 several members and groups within the children's rights lobby immediately issued threats of legal action to the Family Education Trust and to all sections of the media in order to stifle publicity, demanding that the book should be withdrawn from circulation. These threats, however, were based on either trivial detail or misreading of the text and they were not pursued. While much of the media was cautious, the *Daily Telegraph* gave extensive coverage to the story and for this courageous action the author, publisher and, indeed, the general public owe the editor a debt of gratitude. A tremendous demand was stimulated in the UK and other English-speaking countries and it quickly sold out. This new edition adds a number of revelations which have come to light since the book was first published.

By far the most important fact to have emerged is the extent to which the whole 'children's rights' issue is a front behind which the increasingly authoritarian ambitions of certain minority groups, both in this country and in Europe, seek to deprive us of the liberties which adults – not just parents – have taken for granted over many generations.

The evidence of the countless individuals who have contacted us since the book was published has made very apparent just what has been lost over the last few years under the guise of 'children's rights' and how government directives have contributed to this situation. In focusing on the disasters brought upon schools, neighbourhoods, children's homes and families by children's rights initiatives, we came to realise that we were looking at only half the picture. Seeing scenes on television of children defiantly baring their buttocks at the police and running wild on housing estates; of television films which showed classrooms wrecked by pupils, with human excreta deposited on the teacher's desk; of large groups of children stoning ambulances and fire engines; of ten year-old children getting contraceptives from clinics without their parents knowledge or consent – to give but a few examples – have thrown a spotlight upon the scandal of what children can now get away with.

The other side of the picture, which has received little publicity or comment, is far more important. It is the question of how, and by whom, a whole range of adult rights was taken away by laws and regulations which purported to be on behalf of 'children's rights' and have left parents powerless to help or defend themselves from unjustified attack. This is the very position, in fact, that children's rights activists find unacceptable for children, but not for adults.

It is the parental state, for example, which has decided that teachers are at the mercy of their worst behaved children. The proposition was never debated in parliament that teachers, parents and any other authority figure, should be considered guilty of any charge made against them by a child – even their own – until they could prove themselves innocent. And that they did not have recourse to 'due process' of law whereby they could defend themselves, with a jury if necessary, and obtain redress if the claim was found to be malicious or time-wasting. Yet these rights – parents' rights – were specifically abrogated under the Children Act 1989 without anyone seeming to notice the implications for justice in this country.

Similarly, the fact that adults are prevented from taking effective measures against hooligans, even in their own front gardens. When was the right to defend oneself or one's property, slyly taken away? This also was never debated in parliament and it has not been replaced with anything else.

And why, for instance, is it only certain causes that are deemed fit to be taken to the European Court? Why is it always homosexual or feminist rights, and the rights of the anti-corporal punishment pressure groups which are given time and money to challenge the law? Why not the right of parents to refuse contraceptives for their children when they are below the legal age of consent? Or the right of schools to determine their own disciplinary procedures?

In short, we would be missing the whole picture if, in looking at what the children's rights activists have achieved and how they have done it, we overlook the extent to which those who govern us are content to see adults intimidated and rendered powerless. The new spirit emanating from 'Europe' is, as we know to our cost, obsessed with control. We should not be surprised that they welcome and encourage children's rights as much as possible. Never before has the bureaucracy had such an entrée into the personal lives of individuals and on such an uncontentiously pious pretext. Whenever we hear the argument pressed for children's rights – which invariably means the right of officials to exercise a planned 'right' on their behalf – we should pay far more attention to the established adult right that is being obliterated in its name.

This new edition includes all the information of the original document, together with much new material. It would be worthwhile for the reader to take note of those occasions, even if not directly referred to, when government, with the wide range of pressure groups to choose between, singles out the children's rights lobby for support. And to ask the question, what inconvenient power of the individual, the family, or the community was, thereby, removed without protest.

Lynette Burrows identifies three particular interest groups who wish to undermine the strength of the family. First is the commercial sector which welcomes the availability of young people, particularly girls, as a market for products which would be unsuitable to their age and stage of development if the law on the age of consent were to be taken seriously.

Secondly, there are those who wish to see parental rights removed, in respect to their ability to protect and discipline their children as they think fit. This group wants to gain sexual access to young people for personal and ideological reasons that may often be inextricably bound up together. They often have an intense dislike of the traditional family because they see it as oppressive and paternalistic. On the other hand, some also want young people to be sexually available to them. Chapter five indicates that the second motive has been more significant than the first in developments to further paedophile objectives.

Third and last, the most oppressive of all the forces ranged against the family, is that of state-employed professionals. It is they who have the twin incentives of power and money to attract them to waging a war on the territory previously governed by parents. This works in two ways. In effect they are paid to over-ride parents by helping children to seek contraceptive advice behind their backs, or to place themselves in local authority care, for example. Then they are paid to try to solve any problems which result from their earlier interference, such as sexually transmitted disease, pregnancy, abortion, homelessness and drug-dependence. This is not to say that state employees are alone in creating the factors which propel children into disaster, but it is to draw attention to the less than helpful effect of alienating and marginalizing parents – who should be the first line of defence in protecting children from harm.

It is professionals who have persuaded a largely well-meaning but often ill-informed media that they know so much more about child rearing than parents do, and that parents should be obliged to go to them to learn 'parenting skills'.

This is particularly surprising considering that in September 1998 the Social Services Inspectorates issued a report which pointed out the extent to which local authorities fail to look after the children in their care. The health minister, Frank Dobson, commented that though children in care represented only 0.5% of the country's children, they came to form an extremely high proportion of young people in real trouble. The report shows that 22% of the prison population is made up of young men who have been in care, including 39% of prisoners under the age of 21. One-third of the people sleeping rough in London have been in care. Add to this the large number of cases of child abuse which take place in Local Authority children's homes, and you will begin to wonder how any organisation which claims to have the interest of children at heart can possibly initiate measures which can only result in more children going into care.[1]

One would think that all this was evidence enough that professionals come a very poor second to most parents when it comes to the bringing-up of children. It is ironic, therefore, that there should be continual pressure from the government and its agencies for parents to attend classes on parenting, given by professionals – it may be more appropriate for professionals to attend classes run by experienced and successful parents, rather than by the inexperienced idealogues who currently train them. Professionals have shown themselves repeatedly, and for a long time, to be inadequate for the job of parent-substitute; but this has not prevented them from seeking – and getting – ever more power over parents.

There is perhaps no clearer example of professionals taking over the territory properly occupied by parents than the behaviour of the children's rights movement. As Lynette

---

[1] 'Don't taxpayers care about children in care?' Minette Marrin, *Daily Telegraph* 24.9.98

Burrows convincingly demonstrates in her remarkable book, this scarcely deserves to be regarded as a 'movement' at all. It was started by a few individuals who formed a succession of front organisations, who asked each other to sit on committees, took 'evidence' from each other, and produced 'reports'. Because of their uncritical treatment by the media, it goes unremarked that these organisations have nothing by way of grass-roots membership or popular support. Their income is derived from government departments and a couple of grant-making trusts. To put it bluntly, without Peter Newell as founder and co-ordinator of the various groups and the Calouste Gulbenkian Foundation and the Joseph Rowntree Charitable Trust which have largely provided the funds, the children's rights agenda would simply disappear. The situation is clearly illustrated in the Appendix.

Given the stated aims of the paedophile movement which Lynette Burrows reveals, we should be particularly wary of permitting any steps which could undermine the ability of parents to protect their own children. She shows how in the heady days of the 'sexual revolution', paedophiles were able to present themselves as just another persecuted minority and then cleverly hitched their bandwagon to the more popular cause of 'gay rights'. For a while it looked as if they might have some chance of achieving their objectives but, for a variety of reasons, we are currently in the midst of an unprecedented backlash against paedophiles which puts them at risk wherever they live. If there was ever any public sympathy for their aims, it has long since evaporated.

The need to protect children from the attentions of those who would harm and corrupt them has never been so keenly felt. Yet it would appear that some people in influential quarters are still prepared to accommodate the demands of organisations which have regularly taken children's rights to mean the right of children to be liberated from their parents who by the nature of things provide the most effective obstacle to the excessive power of the state.

It is therefore of the utmost importance for decision makers to review and revise their policies and laws in keeping with the real interests and needs of children and of all those parents who seek to protect them from exploitation and corruption.

Valerie Riches
Director, Family Education Trust
Oxford, February 1999

Chapter 1

The Progress of a Peculiar Ideology

The general public is being seriously misled in the matter of 'children's rights'. For most people, the idea of rights for children centres on their welfare: the need to protect them from harm and to provide them with the basic necessities of life. It would never occur to them that this necessary and benign intention is being misused by those who want to change the family from what they see as a bourgeois, paternalistic, oppressive institution to a new, radical activity unit where parents are merely caretakers of children, on sufferance from the state.

Most people would probably agree with the United Nations Convention on the Rights of the Child when it speaks of the family being the 'fundamental group of society' and that children should be afforded the 'necessary protection and assistance' to enable them to grow up in 'a family environment, in an atmosphere of happiness, love and understanding'.[1] That is indeed what parents in general have always sought for their children and have, in most cases, devoted the major part of their lives to achieving. It is an entirely uncontentious statement — until you see how it can be interpreted.

Consider this statement of intent, issued by an organisation called the Children's Rights Office in June 1995:

> Traditionally, there has tended to be a presumption that parents' rights prevail until children can demonstrate a capacity for exercising their rights. But the obligation in Article 5 [of the UN Convention] to act 'in a manner

consistent with the evolving capacities of the child' suggests that the presumption should be reversed: parents should exercise their rights to over-ride the actions of a child only where the child is not competent to understand fully the consequences of their actions, or where failure to intervene would place the child at risk or would cause harm to, or interfere with, the rights of others.[2]

The thing to be noted here is the spin being put on the innocent-sounding observation that parents should 'act in a manner consistent with the evolving capacities of the child'. Most parents, of course, do act in this manner because they love their children and want to give them what they need, provided it is in their best interest; but now, it is suggested, this is not enough. It is being suggested instead that others, outside the family, should supersede the right of parents to rear their children as they think fit, and that they, and not parents, should decide when a child is 'competent'.

The platitudinous nature of the wording of the Convention identifies it as belonging to a familiar sub-language beloved of government employees, and the know-all tone is its hallmark. It would be laughable, if it were not so serious, that a group of bureaucrats/politicians should set themselves up to preach to the majority of their fellow-citizens about something so basic as how to rear their children. However, notwithstanding their almost ludicrous effrontery in this matter, the implications for family life are serious.

The assumption that there is a right way of bringing up all children and that the experts at the Children's Rights Office, alone, know what it is, should warn us that we are in the company of zealots with 'alternative', if undeclared, ideas about what constitutes the correct way for parents to behave with their children.

There is a further, disturbing, aspect of the campaign for the hoped-for legislation on children's rights which is revealed in the language of the proponents. It seeks to pit the interests of the child against those of parents on the principle of 'divide and rule'. Parents are assumed to be hostile to the interests of their children until proved otherwise. Social workers, on the other hand, labour under no such demeaning assumption.

To most reasonable people, it would appear bizarre to assume that normal, responsible parents, who bear, raise and love their children, are less to be trusted than those who merely earn a living from them – but this is, indeed, the stance of the children's rights movement. They assume that there is something in the very nature of parenthood which is inimical to the interests of children; which holds them back and over-protects them, to their detriment.

Though they have to admit that children are vulnerable by virtue of being children, they nevertheless believe that this vulnerability is caused in the first place by parental attitudes. Here is Gerison Lansdown, Chair of the Children's Rights Development Unit, writing in the handbook *Children's Participation in Decision Making* in 1995:

> Much of children's vulnerability derives from historical attitudes and presumptions about the nature of childhood and is a social and political construct and not an inherent or inevitable consequence of childhood itself . . . it is as much the structures within which children have to live which serve to render them vulnerable.[3]

The handbook goes on to say that 'the predominance of a protective model in the construction of our relationships with children' has inhibited them from developing their full capacity. This highly questionable assertion is then used as the basis for establishing 'children's rights' – which children can use to defend their own vulnerability!

We must be clear about this since it is the nub of their argument and the driving force behind all their ideas. They believe that the accumulated experience of generations of parents is faulty and has, indeed, always been so. The proposal is to substitute an experiment where parents are marginalised as the principal protectors and educators of their children and professionals from outside the family are brought in to do the job. Obviously, the fact that these professionals will be unencumbered by a desire to protect the children from what the parents would consider harmful, is part of the appeal of the proposals.

Being largely untried and ideological, there is no track-record to go on when considering the likely outcome of such a massive social experiment; nor, of course, is there public acquiescence. We have only the inadequate credentials of the people who are advancing these ideas to validate them – which is no doubt why they are at such pains to create an impression of impregnable scientific respectability as well as of wide-spread professional and public support. The media which, by and large, knows little of the subject has given uncritical support to what seem to be indisputably 'nice' ideas and have thus helped to perpetuate an illusion that the movement for 'children's rights' is both intellectually well-grounded and widely supported. As we shall see, this is not the case.

Chapter 2

Weaving the Web

It is obvious to anyone that the whole area of children's rights opens up vast new career opportunities for those involved, with the added attraction of the power it would bestow to interfere in the lives of others. It is unlikely to be coincidental that the keenest advocates of the new rights lobby are officials who are already active in childcare services. The power-base of the movement is almost entirely bureaucratic and institutional: individual support, in either time or donations, is conspicuous by its absence. This is a movement which pits the power of institutions against families, and aims to weaken the right of the family to conduct its own affairs without interference from outside bodies.

The condescending, and indeed, insulting attitude to parents, has echoes in everything produced by the children's rights movement. In introducing the Children Act 1989, which embodies so many of their aims and attitudes, the former Lord Chancellor, Lord Mackay – perhaps unwittingly – caught the tone exactly:

> the days when a child should be regarded as a possession of his parent . . . are now buried forever. The overwhelming purpose of parenthood is the responsibility of caring for, and raising the child to be a properly developed adult, both physically and morally.[4]

One has to ask Lord Mackay where he got the idea that this patronising comment would be a new insight to most parents. What is in the least bit new about his sentiments except for the stark fact that the power to define that responsibility, and to decide what constitutes the proper development of a child into an adult, is taken away from parents and given to social workers and others?

Here is Gerison Lansdown again: 'the family is no longer considered without question a secure, safe and stable environment for all children'.[5] She continues by citing the current problems facing the family, which she does not identify as having been caused largely by the breakdown of the traditional family and its replacement with looser, alternative lifestyles. Instead, she sees the breakdown of the family as inevitable or already accomplished, and uses this as the justification for the complete destruction of this archaic institution:

> A model of parents as holders of all rights and responsibilities in respect of children is no longer accepted as either possible or desirable.[6]

One might ask by whom it is no longer accepted, except that one knows the answer: children's rights activists.

A little band of activists

It is appropriate at this juncture, therefore, to examine in more detail the organisation of these activists, to see if there is any common thread which links them and accounts for the concerted action which has brought them so much success.

The first thing to notice is that there are, in fact, very few of them, although they have given an impression of an army with banners. It is necessary therefore to examine more closely the *dramatis personae* of the movement in order to understand how it has been organised and how it operates with so little opposition.

There are currently seven children's rights organisations up and running, with an eighth now defunct because it has served its purpose (see Appendix). All of them have been founded or co-founded by Peter Newell. He is a pressure-group leader *par excellence* and his skills and dedication have pushed along 'children's rights' in their present form, from the first.

His career with 'rights' organisations began as Rights Education Officer, funded by the Gulbenkian Foundation, at the National Council for Civil Liberties, and as director of the Advisory Centre for Education. Both of these organisations were radical, left-wing and much involved with a whole range of other 'rights' organisations.

Peter Newell then moved on to become one of the original directors of the Children's Legal Centre (CLC), set up in 1979 as an extended project of the International Year of the Child. This organisation started life with £15,000 from the DHSS and nearly £12,000 from the Rowntree Charitable Trust. In the five years for which annual reports have been submitted to the Charity Commission government departments have contributed £165,000 of taxpayers' money to the organisation and the Rowntree Charitable Trust has contributed £122,000.

In 1985, the Children's Legal Centre unsuccessfully petitioned the House of Lords to be granted the status of *amicus curiae* to represent children in the Gillick case. whereby doctors were allowed to prescribe the pill for girls under 16 without their parents' knowledge or consent. The CLC had been vocal throughout in favour of taking away the right of parents to know what their under-age daughters were contemplating in terms of serious sexual commitment and, when the Lords decided in favour of the family planning lobby, the centre rejoiced that:

> The Victorian concept of absolute parental authority and control has been replaced by the new concept of partnership between parents and children. The power of the parent dwindles and the power of the child increases as the child grows in years and understanding.[7]

This was a little presumptuous in view of the fact that it is not, so far, enshrined in primary legislation and, indeed, was modified somewhat in a later case which allowed parents to insist on treatment for a child even without its consent.

In 1985 Newell moved sideways from the CLC to become treasurer of the Society of Teachers Opposed to Physical Punishment (STOPP). This organisation successfully campaigned for the abolition of corporal punishment in schools in 1986, in the teeth of opposition from a large proportion of the teaching profession, parents and children themselves. An unwary parliament passed the legislation by one vote following an earlier decision by the European Court which might well have made it inevitable anyway. The European Court ruled (in Campbell & Cosans v. UK) that the philosophical convictions of parents with regard to corporal discipline in schools must be respected. It did not follow that *all* corporal punishment in schools had to be abolished; merely that the views of parents opposed to it should be respected with regard to their own children. However, as usual, the UK interpreted this advice along doctrinaire lines.

Having achieved its objective, STOPP transferred its funds to a new organisation which would campaign for legislation forbidding the use of any form of physical discipline in any setting, including the family. End Physical Punishment of Children (EPOCH), with its linked charity, the Association for the Protection of All Children (APPROACH), was launched in 1989 with Newell as coordinator of both, and his domestic partner, mother of his children and until recently the Principal Policy Officer of the National Children's Bureau, Rachel Hodgkin, as a director of both.

Chapter 3

Exploding the Myth of 'Widespread Support'

In the impressive manifesto of EPOCH, sixty childcare organisations were listed as supporters, including the Children's Legal Centre. However, in 1997, Families for Discipline (a parents' group set up to uphold the rights of parents to exercise and delegate physical discipline for their own children) published an article by Nicola Wells, a London mother who had written to each of the 44 organisations on EPOCH's list with offices in England and Wales and asked them three questions:

1. At what level in their organisation was the anti-smacking policy agreed?
2. On what research was it based?
3. Did their opposition to smacking extend to supporting legislation against loving parents smacking their own children?

Mrs Wells received 39 replies, representing 80% of EPOCH's support in England and Wales. Of the total, one group could not be traced and a further two either shared personnel or premises with EPOCH. Two of the organisations stated quite emphatically that they did not agree with EPOCH's aims. One of these, the Professional Association of Nursery Nurses (PANN), said they had written to EPOCH in 1994 asking that their name be withdrawn. It wasn't. PANN had earlier individually balloted its members on the question of smacking and received an overwhelmingly negative response to adopting EPOCH's position.

It is important to note that none of the other groups who replied to Mrs Wells' letter had canvassed grass-roots opinion within their organisation on the matter of parental discipline. Those who had been through any consultation process at all had left the policy decision to executive members, committees or annual general meetings where only a handful of the membership were represented.[8]

Typical of this approach was the National Childminding Association (NCMA) which had informed *The Guardian* that it had formally adopted a 'no smacking' policy in 1990 and that its members had overwhelmingly endorsed the position. In fact, it had never individually balloted its 50,000 members on the issue at all. The vote was taken on a resolution which was tabled at the AGM itself, so very few were prepared for it. Fewer than five hundred delegates were present, which is 1% of all their membership and 0.5% of all childminders nationwide and they block-voted on behalf of the rest.[9]

A 1992 survey of childminders in the Sutton area by Anne Davis of Families for Discipline revealed that, of the few NCMA members who had been subsequently balloted by the Association, 94% believed that an occasional smack was an effective disciplinary tool, and 69% said they would be willing to smack a minded child if the Department of Health relaxed its guidelines.[10] This is ironic since the Department explained that it had altered its policy of permitting parents to delegate the power to smack their child to others precisely because of the representations made to it by groups like the National Childminding Association, which claimed to have consulted its members on the matter. The Department also ventured the observation that 'some research suggests that physical punishment may not be a very effective sanction'.

When asked to identify the source of this research, the Department referred to EPOCH! [11]

Where is the research?

In answer to Mrs Wells' second question about which research they had relied on in order to come to their decision, only five organisations cited any research whatsoever and all of these related to physical and sexual abuse rather than to parental discipline. Many of the organisations listed also referred to EPOCH as the source of their 'research', which is a circular movement indeed! Typical of these was the Chair of the Children and Families Committee of the influential Association of Directors of Social Services, who wrote: 'I think you would find all the information you need most easily available from an organisation called EPOCH . . . '

Several organisations were refreshingly honest and admitted they had not used any research as a basis for their support of EPOCH. A typical response was from Defence for Children International who explained the unanimous support of his committee for EPOCH in these terms:

> It was disparate rather than common persuasion. I think other committee members at the time may have reacted emotively rather than informedly.

Interestingly, this little-known group was more involved in the drafting and monitoring of the UN Convention on the Rights of the Child than any other non-governmental organisation.

Also very honest was the Chair of the Children and Families Sub-committee of the British Association of Social Workers, who said:

> We are not aware of any research which demonstrates that children who have received physical punishment fare better or worse than others . . . Given this 'not proven either way' position, however, we do believe that the onus of proof should be on those who favour smacking. [12]

This is clearly wrong since, given that 90% of parents in the UK have consistently been found to believe smacking is necessary, the onus of proof should be on those who disagree to prove their position, rather than the other way round. However, it is extremely significant that, even at this level, it is admitted that there is no research evidence to substantiate their beliefs. This is quite contrary to the claims constantly made by EPOCH. Who can doubt that if there were any real research evidence, they would have used it themselves?

The most prestigious member of the EPOCH Board is undoubtedly Dr Penelope Leach, who, although not a medical doctor as many believe, is a psychologist and widely-known childcare specialist. In May 1993 she set out the case against smacking children in *The Psychologist,* the magazine of the British Psychological Society, and was criticised in the September issue of the same publication by Professor Hans Eysenk, professor of psychology at the Institute of Psychiatry. Quoting her statement that 'the use of physical punishment frequently provokes or exacerbates behaviours parents and others wish to minimise', he asked: 'How can we know this?'

He pointed out that her proposition was only one of three possibilities, the other two being that

- there was a strong genetic element in both the child's misbehaviour and the parents' reaction to it; and
- that it was the child's unacceptable behaviour, however caused, which caused the parent to adopt a punitive strategy.

Adopting only one possibility as if it had been proved was, he said, 'not acceptable scientifically'. He went on to say: 'Psychologists should be chary of giving advice not based on rigorous research evidence . . . Leach's account is too one-sided to form the basis of responsible recommendations to law-giving bodies'.[13] So much for EPOCH's claim to be scientifically well grounded.

As a matter of fact, there is research evidence on this subject that has been carefully evaluated by a non-partisan body, the Family Research Council* in America. Its edition for October 1996 was called 'Spare the Rod': New Research Challenges Spanking Critics, and it covered, amongst other things, a survey by the National Institute of Healthcare Research, which had looked into the research literature on corporal punishment. It found that 83% of the 132 identified articles published in clinical and psychological journals were merely opinion-driven editorials, reviews or commentaries, devoid of new empirical findings.

Moreover, most of the empirical studies were methodologically flawed by grouping the impact of abuse with spanking. 'The best studies demonstrated beneficial, not detrimental, effects of spanking in certain situations.'

In addition, they record that 70% of paediatricians believe there is no connection between loving parental chastisement and child-abuse and that, 'Remarkably, childhood aggression has been more closely linked to maternal permissiveness and criticism than to even abusive physical discipline.'

They also cite research evidence which indicates that teaching parents appropriate spanking may actually reduce child abuse, a finding which is born out in the Swedish situation. It quotes a 1995 report from the Swedish government organisation 'Statistics Sweden', which says that reports of child abuse have risen four-fold from 1984 to 1994. (smacking was banned in 1979). During the same period reports of teen violence have risen six-fold. Our own experience follows this closely since child-abuse and juvenile violence has increased in inverse proportion to the pressure brought to bear on parents to eschew loving chastisement.

*Family Research Council, 700 Thirteenth St N W, Suite 500, Washington D C 20005.   Tel: 202-393-2100.

Turning parents into criminals

It was on the question concerning legislation against parents who smacked their children that the replies were most interesting. The National Childminding Association, the Association of Metropolitan Authorities, the Day Care Trust and the National Association of Nursery Nurses, for example, all had no view on the matter of legislating against parental smacking and many others echoed the British Association of Social Workers' view that: 'Certainly parental smacking of a limited and caring kind should not be criminalised'.

Even Childline said it 'takes no position on whether smacking can be the subject of legislation', and Save the Children Fund recognises that this is not an issue to be addressed by legislation. In the end, the number of organisations unambiguously favouring legislation did not even reach double figures. Therefore, EPOCH's claim that the sixty listed organisations support their aim to 'end all physical punishment by education and legal reform' is misleading to say the least.[14]

In November 1998 Barnardo's published a campaigning leaflet, *Children are Unbeatable,* listing over 160 organisations in support of EPOCH's campaign to make parents who smack their children subject to the charge of criminal assault. The address given was that of EPOCH. To launch itself on a national scale EPOCH needed nationally recognised names. It also needed nationwide support. These requirements were supplied by the Alliance Strategy Group, headed by five organisations: Barnardo's, NCPCC, Save the Children, the National Children's Bureau and, of course, EPOCH.

A survey based on a sample of 956 adults carried out by Opinion Research Business in December 1998 showed that only 13% of respondents thought all forms of physical punishment should be outlawed. Of those, nearly a fifth had smacked their children and a further third were childless. Because of the consistency of previous polls in showing that between 80% and 90% of parents would not support the aims of the Alliance, the question of membership support of executive committee decisions has to be raised yet again. One wonders whether Safeways, for example, consulted their staff and their customers before allowing their name to be associated with a campaign of this nature?

It is also interesting that of the 160 names on the list 82 have been in receipt of funds over the past four years from the Calouste Gulbenkian Foundation, one of the main benefactors of the children's rights movement. Of those 160 names some 22 can be directly connected by personnel or funding to EPOCH and the Children's Rights Office. Moreover of those 160 names, 13 are duplications or branches of organisations already listed or funded by the Joseph Rowntree Charitable Trust. Disregarding the few names with no addresses and the five Alliance Strategy Group names, the support is diminished by at least 50%. How much less would there be if the members of all the organisations had been consulted?

It is also instructive to notice the ludicrous, if unconscious, assumption of superiority with which they solemnly assume that the opinions of 160, or even 500, 'professional' people are more impressive than millions of ordinary people who think differently. We are talking about childcare here, not some abstruse science, and the opinions and experience of ordinary parents are just as valid as anybody else's. The attempt to put childcare beyond their intellectual range is so destructive of their confidence and wellbeing that one can only wonder at the heedless conceit that has promoted the attempt. Those interested in how other countries have supposedly fared with this policy, should refer to the chapter which specifically deals with Sweden.

Strengthening the campaign

Peter Newell set up and became Chair of the Children's Rights Development Unit. This followed a two-day seminar in London in 1992 promoted by EPOCH, and called 'Ending Physical Punishment of European Children'.

From this organisation came the Children's Rights Office, which is a project of the Development Unit with charitable status. It too has Peter Newell and his partner, Rachel Hodgkin, on its Board. The annual report explains that, in the absence of any real reform towards the implementation of the Convention, the Children's Rights Office plans to 'strengthen the campaign for a Children's Rights Commissioner'.[15]

To bolster this initiative, he used APPROACH, a charity linked to EPOCH, which had received over £400,000 in charitable trust money between 1989 and 1995, with Newell, Hodgkin and Penelope Leach as directors. Together with Martin Rosenbaum, formerly of the Children's Legal Centre, he published *Taking Children Seriously: A proposal for a Children's Rights Commissioner* in 1991.

This report was published by the Calouste Gulbenkian Foundation which had contributed an average of £13,000 a year to APPROACH since its inception in 1989 as well as contributing to the other Peter Newell creation, the Children's Legal Centre. During the same period the Joseph Rowntree Charitable Trust contributed more than £230,000 to APPROACH.

Most recently of all, we have the case involving a stepfather who beat his son for what the child's mother described as desperately bad behaviour. The father was cleared of assault in the British court, but the case was taken to the European court by people interested in securing a judgement to weaken parental authority.

Those interested in the progress and techniques of these

ideologues will note that the presence, representing the boy, of Alan Levy QC, with Peter Newell as 'Official Advisor' to the boy's legal team. Alan Levy, in the past, had been either a legal advisor or a member on three of the four 'reports' funded by the Calouste Gulbenkian Foundation and produced, very largely, by Peter Newell and his associates. For example, he was a member of the 1995 'commission' on 'Children and Violence' which comprised Peter Newell as research coordinator, with no fewer than twelve of the seventeen members of the commission being associated with EPOCH, either as personal sponsors – as in the case of Sir William Utting, chairman of the commission – or as senior officers in organisations which had publicly identified themselves with the cause of making parental discipline illegal.

A further fascinating example of the serpentine inter-relations between a handful of individuals and organisations is provided by the Calouste Gulbenkian Foundation itself. Based in Portugal, this organisation is not accountable in the UK. It is known that the current director of its UK branch, Ben Whitaker, was Director of the Minority Rights Group of the NCCL, and stood for election to the National Executive. Peter Newell was the Education Officer of the same organisation, his office funded by the Calouste Gulbenkian Foundation.

Its Deputy Director is Paul Curno, a former residential worker, childcare officer and social work trainer. He was formerly Secretary of the Children's Rights Office, whose aim is to achieve the appointment of a Children's Rights Commissioner. He resigned his directorship and his position as Company Secretary of the Children's Rights Development Unit and the Children's Rights Office in May 1997. This is just as well because there would seem to be a considerable conflict of interest in a person disbursing funds to the tune of at least £93,000 to five organisations in which he has a prominent role.

However, he continues as Deputy Director (UK) of the Gulbenkian Foundation Their involvement and funding of the current children's rights activity, particularly within the 'European' context and at the United Nations, must have played a major part in the success so far of the movement. It has also funded seven out of eight of Peter Newell's various organisations since 1976 when it gave nearly £10,000 to the first London Free School.

This is not an unimportant matter since what is influencing public policy regarding the family is a matter of genuine interest and the public has a right to know both who is funding powerful pressure groups and on what basis.

That there is an element of ideological bias in the children's rights agenda at present is fairly obvious from their targets, achievements and pronouncements so far. From the point of view of the public, nothing but good can come from a more frank and open discussion of the people involved, their inter-related organisations, and their real goals in the field of childcare.

A small but significant example of the operation of this ideological driving force is the attempt to increase the right of homosexuals to foster and adopt children. It is well-known that the public is implacably opposed to any such liberalisation of fostering practice on the entirely unprejudiced grounds that a child needs both a mother and a father and that, in trying to place an already disadvantaged child with a substitute family, maximum consideration should be given to this fact. This is so obvious that it falls within the example of 'King Solomon's Ring. Any mother who would make her child suffer, in order to claim her right to it, is not fit to have care of that child.

Yet there are some social services departments who not only ignore this basic right of children to have a parent of either sex in their foster home, but force the child to be the innocent means by which they achieve their ideological ends. It is the child which they use as a battering-ram to break down the prejudices of society and most people would consider this a flagrant breach of the child's right to be placed in an uncontentious family background.

Chapter 4

Children's Rights Triumphant

In the round-up of what a dedicated group of campaigners has been able to achieve, we should not overlook their decisive contribution to the Children Act of 1989. Many of the personnel of the various organisations were and are also members of various government advisory bodies. The resulting Act contains almost everything they could have wished for and bears the hallmark of their anti-parental bias.

The practical result of this Act has meant that a rebellious child can appeal to a social worker to escape the care and control of its parents, even when that care and control is entirely in the interests of the child. There are now many cases of children putting themselves into council care in order to escape the reasonable discipline of their parents. These children have, all too often, gone completely off the rails thereafter, to the anguish of their parents and to all who love and really care for them.

Police and social services personnel are obliged by the Children Act to allow children's wants to prevail even when they know it is not the best thing for them. It has caused much anguish and trouble, not only to thousands of families who find themselves unable to exercise authority over their children, but also in schools where teachers are afraid to lay even a restraining hand on children. Everyone who deals with children has now run up against the proscriptive provisions of this Act which effectively turns responsible adults into ineffectual spectators of the bad and self-destructive behaviour of countless children who need to be controlled. These adults did not for the most part abdicate their authority; it was taken from them by the interpretation put upon an Act which was designed to do just that.

Where does it come from?

So finally, one comes to the question of why and how this peculiar, undemocratic and unnatural belief in 'children's rights' came to life when it did. We can see how children's rights have been insinuated into mainstream debate by careful marketing and assiduous promotion by a very few individuals, acting over many years in concert. But what is the source of these beliefs?

It is fairly uncontentious to say that they are left-wing, and in some cases even Marxist. Communist regimes do not like the family because it is autonomous and influences and protects children whom the state wishes to propagandise and use for its own ends. In his book *Children Are People Too* (reprinted by APPROACH in 1992) Peter Newell quotes, without irony, the fact that the Soviet Union abolished corporal punishment in school in 1917 and that they regarded it as 'not merely ineffective but harmful'. Not as effective as the Gulag, anyway, and somewhat less harmful, one might add.

He also quotes approvingly some purblind 'expert' who discovered that there was 'very little child abuse or neglect in China', where they had also abolished corporal punishment. The level of serious inquiry here speaks for itself.

It is noticeable that, within the field of children's rights, the question of a conceived child's right to be born is never raised. Although it can fairly be described as a fundamental right which should at least be considered by anybody seriously interested in the subject, it has received no attention whatever from the movement.

Neither has the right of children to have both a father and a mother, rather than being planned and conceived by artificial means to satisfy the entirely selfish desire of single people and homosexual couples to have children. It is the children's rights activists who set the agenda by means of their organisations and few seem to realise how specifically radical and ideological their interests are.

However, this blindness about the ideological blueprint they have been furnished with is typical of many politically naive people – which is no doubt why Lenin called them naïve. What has been forgotten is that it was in the 1970s that talk of 'children's rights' really got under way in their modern, non-welfare, sense and that many of the people driving it were paedophiles and their associates in the 'civil rights' industry, who were working for homosexual equality.

Chapter 5

The Rainbow Connection

In the 1970s paedophiles were, in some circles, considered an uncontentious minority group whose needs should be catered for. Indeed, just how uncontentious they were considered, is indicated by the fact that such luminaries as Professor Freddie Ayres, Baroness Wooton and Jo Richardson MP sent letters of support to the Paedophile Information Exchange (PIE) when they ran a campaign against corporal punishment in schools. PIE was an affiliated member of the National Council of Civil Liberties and it remained a member until it was officially prosecuted and finally suppressed in 1982.

Paedophilia was considered at that time as just one aspect of 'homosexual rights' and it took a number of years for bitter experience to produce the present fear and revulsion of it.

Initially it was paedophiles who wanted 'children's rights' because they wanted sexual access to children. It seems incredible to us now, but the idea was regarded as quite legitimate and many respectable people were quite happy to be non-judgemental about paedophile activists. The Family Planning Association's attitude towards homosexuality has long been that it is as natural and normal as heterosexual intercourse in their booklet *Learning to Live with Sex*, for 13 - 16 year olds.[16] However, in 1970 it was recommending a book called *Boy, Girl, Man, Woman* which contained this remarkable professional advice:

> As a rule 'enticers' [of young children] are kindly people who treat children tenderly and affectionately and the child's natural sexual curiosity may find an outlet in the company of paedophiles. If the child lacks warmth and

37

love in his or her home, the recognition of such feelings in the 'enticer' will make him or her feel secure and comfortable in his company.[17]

From 1974 when the Paedophile Information Exchange was formed in Scotland, until 1981 when it was prosecuted for 'conspiring to corrupt public morals', (not, be it noted, for presenting a threat to children) paedophiles not only spelled out their aims and objectives, but also described the process by which they could be achieved.

Abolishing the age of consent

Knowing that they were unlikely to get anywhere by arguing for the right of adults to have sex with children, they decided to approach 'liberalisation' from the other end. Paedophile activist Roger Moody expressed it thus in 1976:

> Specifically, this means we don't work to lower the age of consent, but to abolish it, and we don't argue that rights over kids be transferred from courts to parents, but that the only people who have the right to kids' rights are the kids themselves.[18]

From here a strategy developed. The Secretary of the Paedophile Information Exchange produced the first of three broadsheets on *Childhood Rights* which called for the abolition of corporal punishment in schools. By the late 1970s the Paedophile Information Exchange couched all its arguments in terms of children's rights.

The National Council for Civil Liberties advertised in *Childhood Rights,* and in 1976 published a paper entitled *Sexual Offences: Evidence to the Criminal Law Revision Committee,* written by Dr Michael Schofield (a sociologist, not a medical doctor) in which he referred to an earlier work of his where he had advocated abolishing the laws of consent for both boys and girls and the laws against incest, as soon as public opinion allowed.[19]

To substantiate his case, Schofield quoted the Dutch Speijer Report: 'homosexual experiences might benefit boys who would later live heterosexual lives'; and goes on to praise paedophiles as 'gentle, fond of children and benevolent'. 'Childhood sexual experiences', he said, 'willingly engaged in with an adult result in no recognisable damage'.[20]

It is of interest that Michael Schofield was also an advisor to the Brook Advisory Centres which has effectively achieved the abolition of the age of consent by persuading the government to allow them to prescribe the pill and other contraceptives to under-age girls. This was not, of course, done by arguing for the abolition of the age of consent on libertarian grounds; still less by arguing in favour of the rights of adults to have sex with children.

Instead it was argued that, since girls were going to have illegal sexual encounters anyway, the state might as well connive at the offence and make sure that no pregnancy resulted. The fact that this argument is not used in the case of under-age smoking, drinking, or drug-taking clearly demonstrates its outrageous partiality and inconsistency.

It is inevitable that child abuse has been just one of the results of the policy since, in many cases, no effort is made by the clinics to discover the circumstances of the child for whom they are prescribing the pill. What is certain, however is that there has been a 500% rise over the past ten years in the number of girls under the age of consent receiving contraceptive advice: 90,000 in all, one in ten of the 13 to 16 year-old age group.[21]

However, the *de facto* abolition of the age of consent for girls is not the end of the story. In 1996 *The Daily Telegraph* referred to a paper written by Dr Malcolm Pike in *The Lancet* which indicated that, for women who start taking the pill under the age of 20, the risk of subsequently developing breast cancer is increased by 50%.[22] This finding was first noted in 1983, two years before the court ruling which allowed young girls to be prescribed the pill, and it is an observation which every study into the subject since then has confirmed. We now know that a considerable number of very young girls have died or been seriously affected by the pill. The parents of just one of these, 14 year-old Caroline Bacon, who died after being given the pill without their knowledge, have formed an association called Parents Against Oral Contraception for Children, which is trying to regain the right of parents to care for their children as they think fit.

Commenting on these ill effects on young girls and the likely effects in the future on women who had been given the pill as teenagers, Dr James Le Fanu observed 'Over the past twenty years, doctors and particularly their leaders and opinion formers, have, on every moral issue, sided consistently with the forces of progress'.[23]

This is obviously so as the ubiquitous Michael Schofield, as Research Director of the Council for Health Education, has been well placed to make his opinions influential. Both personally and through his charity, the Lyndhurst Settlement, he has funded a large number of permissive charities as well as being a founding trustee of Release, the drugs agency which, at one time, shared a mail-box with the Paedophile Information Exchange.

There was literally reams written during this period about children's rights, however many of those campaigning for children's rights unwittingly provided cover for those who had paedophile opportunities in mind.

Tony Smythe, a homosexual rights activist, former General Secretary of the NCCL and seconded by Peter Newell for election to the NCCL National Executive was, according to the Paedophile Information Exchange journal *Magpie* in 1977, helpful enough to suggest that 'he didn't think PIE was the ideal group to champion the cause of children's rights'.

So who should take the initiative? *Magpie* editor, Warren Middleton, supplied the answer:

> It must come from enlightened progressives, scientific research bodies and professional pressure groups; adults whose arguments cannot be damaged or destroyed by an opposition able to claim that they're guided by self-interest. People with the courage to face the wrath of a nation poisoned by Christian attitudes to sex.[24]

Two years later The Children's Legal Centre began its activities with Peter Newell as coordinator. From then on, one sees the policies advocated by the paedophile groups, i.e. children's rights, vigorously pursued by a succession of Peter Newell initiatives. This is not to say that it is a sexual interest in children which has motivated him or all the children's rights activists. Nevertheless, in pursuing the specific rights which had been advocated as being in their interest by paedophiles, the children's rights activists have effectively given them both what they wanted and a cover for those designs.

Chapter 6

Liberating Children

For most of the children's rights activists, it was no doubt the fact that the language of children's rights was couched in socialist terms which appealed to them. However, close collaboration with those who saw 'minority rights' in terms of the freedom of children to be sexually available has influenced their thinking and, more importantly, their agenda.

The homosexual and civil liberties movement are inseparable as to personnel, as were the homosexual and paedophile rights people at one time; and whenever you get talk of 'children's rights' from this group, the subject of sexual rights is never far behind. This is exemplified by Jamie Gough, writing in *Pink Triangles:*

> The liberation of children is thus inseparable from the achievement of socialism . . . Children would not be tied, whether legally or socially, to their biological parents, and parents would no longer have the responsibility for the economic maintenance and social care of their children. Rather, this would be the responsibility of the whole community. This does not mean that children would be in nurseries twenty-four hours a day. Children could be integrated into communal households where they could develop stable relationships with a variety of adults, and where they could choose which adults they wanted to be with.[25]

Paedophile/homosexual activist Michael Licarpa, writing to fellow members of PIE in 1983, follows the same course from non-sexual rights, to sexual ones, with anti-smacking thrown in. The child:

. . . must be free to choose who he/she lives with, to be protected against any form of physical punishment, in school, at home or elsewhere, to have the right to work as well as not to, the right to choose their own friends, whether they be child or adult, and many other rights too numerous to mention here, these are all rights. Children must have as of right their personal freedom, besides just the one right to have sexual and loving relationships with whomever he/she wishes, regardless of sex.[26]

The author of the *Labour Gay Rights Manifesto,* Mike McNair, writing with Jamie Gough, demonstrates the link between feminist hatred of the family, children's rights, homosexuality and socialism in a book entitled *Gay Liberation in the Eighties:*

Children grow up under the power of their parents. As children, any behaviour which is obviously sexual in adult terms is repressed . . . A socialist society would supersede the family household . . . gay people and children should have the right to live together . . . Children and young people should have the right to determine their own sexual lives . . . marriage should be disestablished . . . Women need access to free contraception and abortion facilities; this applies just as much to young women as to 'adults'. Children should be able to divorce their parents . . . It follows from what we have already said that we favour the abolition of the age of consent.[27]

It is a disturbing fact that many of these aims have found their way into public policy in the last few years, mostly in a covert way and often in the name of children's rights. Children divorcing their parents, for example, and children's access to state-provided contraception, the right to put themselves into care and out of the protection of their parents. This has been facilitated by the wording of the Children Act 1989 in particular, with its requirement that children are allowed more say in how they are brought up.

This sounds reasonable until one discovers the interpretation that it is possible to put on it; for instance, that a 13 year-old girl can go and live with a 42 year-old married man and her parents can do nothing about it. *The Mail on Sunday* has had a number of articles which featured the plight of parents who had faced similar problems either caused or exacerbated by the divisive provisions of this Act. The paper quoted the relevant words of the Children Act:

> A local authority may provide accommodation for any child within their area (even though a person who has parental responsibility for him is able to provide him with accommodation) if they consider that to do so would safeguard or promote the child's welfare.

It went on to say,

> If you are a parent, read the 43 words above very carefully – they could ruin your life. They come from clause 20.4 of the Children Act, a piece of legislation with chilling implications for every family in Britain . . . The way they are being interpreted means your child can run away from home, aided and abetted by the State . . . and there is absolutely nothing you can do about it. Rebellious children under the age of sixteen are exploiting clause 20.4. They fall out with their parents, declare themselves homeless and force local social services departments to take them in. They face little or no discipline in council care. Bound by the same Act to 'ascertain the child's wishes above everything else', social workers have become an escape route for disenchanted, rebellious children intent on getting their own way.[28]

This situation is particularly serious when one considers that the net result of its provision – that children can opt to go into care, rather than submit to the protective measures of their parents – has coincided with the discovery of the scale of child abuse in children's homes. Such large numbers of children have had their young lives utterly blighted by what happened to them when in the misnamed 'care' of local authorities that fourteen police forces are currently involved in separate investigations. A police chief described the scale of the abuse as 'staggering'. In 1997, the North Wales Tribunal of Inquiry into the 'wholesale exploitation' of children in care in its homes revealed that twelve boys had committed suicide over a 22 year period, in order to 'escape their paedophile tormentors'.[29]

Malcolm King, chairman of Clwyd's social services committee, said: 'children's homes were a Gulag Archipeligo stretching across Britain – wonderful places for paedophiles but, for the children who suffered, places of unending nightmare'. *The Daily Telegraph* listed eleven men imprisoned for serious offences against boys just in Cheshire, with others elsewhere and with many more cases pending.[30]

Although we now know that many care staff saw and deplored the influx of homosexual, paedophile staff into children's homes, for years they remained silent because the ethic of their profession showed a fashionable bias towards a 'non-judgemental' stance on a person's sexual orientation; and they feared for their jobs if they complained. Indeed, in a report published in May 1995 it was explicitly stated by the independent enquiry into the appalling child abuse scandal in children's homes in Islington:

> 'Positive discrimination' towards homosexuals had serious unintended consequences in allowing some staff to exploit children.[31]

This mild comment encompasses the potentially devastating fact that one of the men involved subsequently died of AIDS. We should be prepared to suffer some 'political incorrectness' in order to prevent such things happening in future. However, we are still hampered by the inability to speak plainly or truthfully on the subject.

I should make it clear at this point that I am not

associating all people of a homosexual disposition with paedophilia. But is does seem that too many of those in authority are unwilling to be realistic about the dangers of allowing those homosexuals who may be paedophiles to exploit their tolerance and gain unfettered access to children.

In some respects it is an insult to all decent homosexuals to be so trusting for fear of offending them. No doubt a majority of them do not approve of child molestation and would be horrified by the suggestion that they might encourage or condone it. Exactly the same can be said of heterosexuals who, nevertheless, are happy to see measures taken to curb access to young girls by men who might want to molest them. It does not reflect badly on all heterosexuals to admit that a minority of them are likely to abuse young girls if they are given half a chance. It is accepted that measures are taken to protect girls and it would not be permitted for a man to take them camping with him unaccompanied, or back home for the night. Likewise, no-one so far has suggested that unmarried men be allowed to foster or adopt young girls. This is realism, not prejudice.

However, homosexuals are given the benefit of the doubt and much of the reason for this is propaganda. It is part of the fog that has been blown in our faces in the last few years, that very few people indeed know that homosexuals are much more likely to molest children than are heterosexuals. Most people are aware that a disproportionate amount of cases of paedophilia they read about in the newspapers concern young boys, but they are prepared to believe what some homosexuals continually stress, that this reflects a 'homophobic' desire to blackguard homosexuals by featuring cases in which they are the villains.

This has been investigated from many points of view in the USA and is not true. The word paedophile is non-gender specific and, for this reason, people who wish to be politically correct are able to be equally non-specific when they refer to the problems of paedophiles in childcare.

They may even be deceived themselves, as in the case of the American Psychological Association which sponsored a work which claimed that 'recognised researchers in the field of child abuse . . . almost unanimously concur that homosexual people are actually *less* likely to approach children sexually'.[32]

This is quite simply misleading. It is obviously true that there are more sexual molesters who are heterosexual since, if one considers absolute numbers, approximately 98% of men are heterosexual. However, if the figures are looked at *proportionally*, then it is indisputably the case that homosexual men are far more likely to molest children than are heterosexuals.

Dr Paul Cameron of the Family Research Institute, Washington DC examined the evidence under three headings:

(a) surveys of child molestation in the general population, which involved questionnaires about whether a person had ever been molested, and by whom

(b) surveys of those caught and convicted of child molestation

(c) what homosexuals themselves have reported

He found the results remarkably consistent. The general survey produced a figure of one-third who had been homosexually molested. Between a fifth and a third of convicted paedophiles were homosexual and between a fifth to a third of surveyed gays 'admitted to child molestation'.

His results were published for 'peer criticism' in *Psychological Reports* 1993, and have been corroborated by many other studies in other countries. Freund and Watson provided the most dramatic corroboration of what many have assumed was pejorative reporting in newspapers, when they published their report in 1992 which found that although homosexuals comprised only 2% of adult men, between 40% and 60% of paedophiles were homosexual and 80% of the victims of paedophilia are boys molested by adult males.[33]

The extent that this bias in favour of the 'non-judgemental' approach to employing homosexuals to care for children was revealed by the enquiry into the above-mentioned children's home in Cheshire, where three out of four of the 'housemasters' in one home were homosexual paedophiles. It was also in evidence in Cambridge, where Keith Laverack, a very senior figure in the Social Services Department and a known deviant, was responsible for the care of hundreds of vulnerable children. He was given an 18 year sentence in March 1997 for buggery and assault of the boys in his care. Many suffered crippling long-term after-effects and their lives were ruined.

Social workers at his trial said they knew that he was a deviant figure but did not speak out because they feared for their jobs. One witness testified that she had been told as much by a superior to whom she had expressed doubts about Laverack. In doing research for this book, I was told by a senior lecturer in social work that, in his opinion, the pursuit of Laverack had been an undeserved witch-hunt. 'He gave those boys a lot of love', he said.

It has remained a largely un-publicised scandal that very many social workers in every area knew what was going on but remained silent for fear of being branded 'troublemakers'. And still we do not really know who was protecting the paedophiles, and why.

Conjuring up phantoms

Perhaps this explains the curious persistence of the rumours of 'satanic' abuse which are widely believed amongst social workers. Despite the fact that these had been exhaustively and fruitlessly investigated by the police in the case of the Nottingham children wrongly seized by the social services department, the NSPCC, for instance, immediately circulated what they called a 'discussion document', indicating that the practice was widespread.

In psychological case-studies, it is not unknown for people to personify one specific thing, which they feel unable to name, in terms of another. An unspeakable and unnatural evil which, for some reason, no-one can identify and confront, is presented instead as a metaphor. In the metaphor of satanic abuse, all the elements of paedophilia are there; the cruelty, the ugliness, the unnaturalness, and the power to silence. It is as if those who knew they would be punished if they spoke out against homosexual/paedophile colleagues decided, perhaps unconsciously, to create a drama by other means.

We saw something of the same phenomenon, perhaps, in the tales of bogus social workers who were reported as trying to gain access to little children in order to sexually abuse them, up and down the country. No one saw these phantom social workers arrive at the house, and they vanished like smoke after the alleged incidents, but hundreds of cases were reported by ordinary people who appeared genuinely convinced of their experience. The police investigated every case before coming to the conclusion that it was a form of 'mass hysteria' with no basis in fact.[34]

We have to accept this assessment, but an underlying reality might well be that it is the fear of faceless professionals entering and violating the home which is being personified in these cases, and that this fear, far from being unfounded, is very real.

Chapter 7

Selective Indignation

If it were not for the bias in favour of homosexual rights, children's rights activists might have been at the forefront of the on-going investigations which have unmasked the grievous exploitation suffered by children in care. In the event, they were never there, just as they have shown themselves to be conspicuously uninterested in many other areas of real concern for families.

The list of what could be done to improve the lot of disadvantaged children is very long and it is instructive to notice just how few genuine efforts are made by children's rights activists to address them. The prevailing ugliness and desolation of so many urban settlements are an obvious target for anyone claiming to have the interests of children at heart and the publicity and pressure that institutionally-funded organisations like the Children's Rights Office could bring to bear in small, quite specific areas is immense, had they chosen to do so.

There are, for example, many problems experienced by children who are deprived because their mothers are obliged to work long hours away from them. They could have campaigned for fiscal changes which allowed mothers a choice as to whether they worked or looked after their children. That such changes are now under consideration owes nothing to the efforts of the children's rights activists.

They could have campaigned for the demolition or re-construction of large housing estates; and they could have taken an authoritative lead in showing parents how to work together to contain estate delinquency and drug-pushers.

And where is the sponsored organisation, equivalent to STOPP and EPOCH, campaigning for the right of children not to be bullied and beaten in schools and neighbourhoods? Where are the children's rights activists when it comes to the problem of what to do with the thousands of children excluded from schools every year because no-one can control them, now that both teachers' and parents' hands are tied? Many are left aimlessly wandering the streets and amusement arcades, often a prey to sexual predators and criminals.

Where indeed! The shocking revelations made in *The Guardian* in April 1997 about the paedophile trade in young boys for homosexual orgies quoted the procurers as saying that the number of young boys excluded from school and absconding from children's homes greatly helped them in finding victims.[35] It's an ill wind, as they say, and to the extent that the Children Act 1989 has led to the breakdown of discipline in schools and elsewhere, its advocates must take a large share of the blame.

In the real world, there are far more important campaigns waiting to be fought on behalf of children and the families struggling to bring them up, but the present children's rights advocates are not the people to do it.

A children's rights commissioner

The children's rights juggernaut rolls on and its organised, institutionally-funded campaigns are the only ones which receive the attention of government. The new Labour administration has agreed to accept the United Nations Convention on the Rights of the Child, and Peter Newell, together with Martin Rosenbaum, an erstwhile colleague from the Children's Legal Centre, have published *Taking Children Seriously: A Proposal for a Children's Rights Commissioner* under the auspices of APPROACH (Association for the

Protection of All Children; an offshoot of EPOCH).[36]

In it, they propose a Children's Rights Commissioner with legal powers to bind government, public and voluntary bodies. The proposals require a Commissioner, created by Act of Parliament, to be equipped with a staff of fifty and a budget of £4 million. The Commissioner would be independent of government and would have the power to make significant interventions in family life. His or her bold independence, without accountability to an elected government or any other limiting principle, signals an ominous future for the family. Even with the UN Convention as a sign-post, the Commissioner is guided by, but not limited to, the already far-reaching principles of this Convention.

It is important for the public to realise the true consequences, unintended or otherwise, of support for children's rights as envisaged by these people. It sounds the death knell for family freedoms. For instance, nowhere among the Commissioner's duties is there a request for parental input, although all other organisations, public and voluntary, are to be consulted. The proposals suggest that, even though the Commissioner is not supposed to handle individual cases, the Commissioner's Office will inevitably receive requests for advice, advocacy and information from children, and adults acting on their behalf. It states: 'Advice should not be given to an adult where this could conflict with the rights of the child concerned'.

What this means is that it would provide opportunity for the Commissioner to determine the best interests of the child. As with the Children Act 1989, children in conflict with their parents could, in the name of their 'rights', put themselves into the care of the local authority and their parents could be refused all information about them. This would not be in order to protect the child but in order to assert its 'rights', as laid down by someone else.

It is clear that these proposals have in mind considerable job opportunities for children's rights activists. 'At a later stage it may be possible if the resources are available and in light of the Commissioner's work so far to add to his/her role - or create separately - a carefully designed local or regional system to receive and investigate children's complaints across a defined range of services, together with a network of advocates to support children in making complaints'.

This statement demonstrates two things clearly. The first is in the passing reference to 'a network of advocates' which will be necessary to enforce measures which do not enjoy popular support. One need look no further for the reason why some lawyers are involved in children's rights, as well as charities and childcare professionals. They all stand to gain in terms of work and extra power. The second thing is the way in which children's rights advocates work bit by bit to erode family rights, replacing them with institutional ones. The 'powers to investigate' are likely to be used by the Commissioner to assist or participate in legal action in his/her own name.

Though these proposals say that this power will only be used in exceptional cases of principle, it is easy to guess that one of those principles will be a law to ban the smacking of children by their parents.

This is certain to be considered overwhelmingly important by Peter Newell and his associates, since no less than four of his eight organisations have been exclusively dedicated to this principle. As the director of the Children's Rights Office has said, 'you must remove the protection of parents in hitting their children before any real changes take place'.[37] Indeed, legislation along these lines in both Sweden and Norway followed upon the setting-up of a Children's Ombudsperson.

Are children's rights anti-child?

In looking more deeply into the mission of children's rights, it can be seen that there is more to it than concern for the protection of children. So many of the measures already adopted under their influence have proved themselves so destructive of children's well-being that one is forced to the conclusion that they are not only anti-family; they are also anti-child.

A moment's reflection would tell most people what a 1996 study into child protection confirmed: that state intervention in family life is feared and loathed by most children more than anything.[38] They are more troubled by the state intervening than they are reassured by the protection offered. Children do not want rights, they want love and protection and, as the study pointed out, the majority of them do not want social workers or anyone else coming into their families and telling their parents they are not behaving properly.

It is precisely the people who demand children's rights who are not respecting the child's right to be left alone, free from state intervention. But then, it is not only the children who suffer when the family's autonomy is breached by hostile strangers, even when they come masquerading as friends to the children. Fear, anxiety and unhappiness spread like a contagion through a family and damage each member's ability to cope with problems. The well-being of each member is as important to the others as it is their own and it does no good to anyone to bring the law crashing down on a family in order to improve the supposed lot of the children in some minor respect.

Considerable damage is done to many families by intrusive social workers looking for evidence that a child has been abused in a way most people would consider trivial. Only the most fanatical and unimaginative ideologues would feel a sense of triumph at a father being hauled before the court and stripping him of all authority in the eyes of his wife and his children. The family is wrecked as surely and perhaps as permanently as if they had been overrun by a marauding army. There can be nothing but tears after the 'caring' professions have been called in pursuit of an infringement of rights that children neither want or need. The threat of tearing the family apart must actually serve, in the end, to make fewer children, rather than more, call for help if they really need it.

The children's rights movement has kept a low profile, not seeking out individual supporters but advancing vast changes in social policy by subtle means. In the past, their strategy has been slowly to erode the rights of parents without anyone noticing. Many of the policy decisions they have directly or indirectly influenced appear, in practice, in so many different agencies, such as the police, the teaching profession and childcare services, that it is easy to think they are spontaneous developments rather than a carefully orchestrated campaign.

The blanket ban on the use of physical correction, which was imposed on all local authority and voluntary organisation foster carers by regulations issued under the Children Act 1989, is a case in point. In January 1989 in the House of Lords, the Lord Chancellor, Lord Mackay, warned that many first-class foster parents and potential foster parents would be lost if they were prevented from administering even the mildest form of corporal discipline to their charges.

This has happened, and Families for Discipline has received complaints from many conscientious and experienced foster carers who have young children of their own and have proved the effectiveness of loving physical correction, who now find themselves obliged to discriminate between their own children and fostered children, if they wish to continue to be foster parents. Others have simply been refused local authority approval unless they signed an undertaking that they would never smack.

In addition to this obstacle being put in the way of prospective foster carers, the British Agencies for Adoption and Fostering has recently drawn attention to the fact that the actual adoption of children is something which many social workers positively deter. Of 40,000 children in care or with foster parents, 10,000 need new families and yet only 2,300 are found new families each year. Overall, the number of adoptions has fallen from 21,000 to its present low level.[39]

Commenting on this, the Adoption Forum, an independent think tank says: 'The present arrangements are failing at great cost to prospective adopters and most of all to children, many of whom linger in local authority care far longer than is in their best interest. Common sense and pragmatism frequently take second place to an overzealous application of theory to everyday situations and the concerns of politically correct decision making'.

Is it unreasonable to think that any organisation which exists for the purpose of upholding 'children's rights' should be at the forefront of any struggle to get children out of children's homes and into a home of their own? Children's rights people do not appear to have shown the slightest interest in the subject as far as can be judged from their public pronouncements. Certainly nothing has been achieved to alleviate the situation, despite the fact that children leaving care are four times more likely than others to be unemployed and sixty times more likely to be homeless. Also, a quarter of the adults in prison were in care at the age of sixteen.

The guidelines which were issued during the summer of 1998 by the then health minister, Paul Boateng, were designed to ease this situation; but they are similar to those issued in 1990, which critics say made very little difference. Local authorities, taking their lead from the Children's Act and their own internal ethic, have continued to block adoptions on what most people would consider frivolous grounds, such as the weight of the prospective parents, having a normal attitude towards discipline, or even because they are too middle class.

One might add, on the other hand, that they have continued to employ as foster parents or adoptive parents, people whom they knew were convicted paedophiles. Community Care 29 May 1997 cites four local authorities where children were placed with a known paedophile who was a member of a fostering and adoption panel in Clwyd. So it is not only fair to say that some social services departments are 'over-zealous in theory' when deciding who is suitable as foster parents, but that they are over-zealous in a particular direction. This gives particular cause for concern.

The shortfall in suitable families produced by these arbitrary policies is very likely a contributory factor, perhaps even a planned one, to the remarkable decision of some local authorities to place already disadvantaged children with homosexual couples. At the very least a child is entitled to a family that is as near the norm as possible and, for most people, not having either a mother or a father is the very worst form of deprivation. To actually plan such a family, rather than have it happen by chance or misfortune, is the very height of irresponsibility – and indeed cruelty. And yet, for some ideologues in local authorities, the unknown effects, not to mention the dangers, of homosexual 'parenting' are a preferable risk when compared to having parents who might occasionally want to smack a child, or who smoke.

Rights activists admit that parents exist to protect children; it is one of the things they dislike and want to change. In consequence, parents have found themselves increasingly marginalised in many areas concerning their children in recent years but have been unable to see it as a concerted attack on their rights as parents. The question is, who do the enemies of the family want to protect children, if and when parents' rights are crushed?

The answer to that is contained quite specifically in children's rights literature. Gerison Lansdown, Director of the Children's Rights Office, writes: 'The onus rests on the parents to *justify* intervention which denies the child autonomy rather than the onus being placed on the child to demonstrate competence'.[40] (emphasis added)

In other words, it doesn't matter how obviously immature and vulnerable the child is, the parents have no right to intervene in what it does, unless they can justify this to any agency that may invoke the law. This is the law – or the interpretation of the law, in the form of the Children Act 1989 – that has sent fathers to a police cell for chastising delinquent sons, allowed young schoolgirls to live with boyfriends, and permitted drug-pushers and pimps to make use of children domiciled in children's homes, where no one has the power to control or protect them.

The other weasel word is 'intervention', which is used here disapprovingly to describe any action a parent may take to control their child or to direct its behaviour.

A warning shot across the bows of parents

It is quite clear, from the writings and actions of children's rights activists, that they are the opposed to such parental rights. For a final insight into the direction in which they hope to push their ideas, we should look at the case of the East Sussex mother who smacked her son with a wooden spoon because he bullied her baby and spat in her face when reprimanded. As a result of her chastising the boy, both her children were placed on the 'at risk' register by her local social services department. The mother re-mortgaged her house and took her case to the High Court in order to have the threat to her children, and the slur on her family, lifted. She lost the case although the judge said there was no question of child abuse in her case and that she was obviously a good mother. When asked to comment on the case as co-ordinator of EPOCH, Peter Newell welcomed the decision and said, 'this is a warning-shot across the bows of all parents'.[41]

This is the authentic threatening voice of the children's rights lobby and it should both frighten and warn all those who have the interests of children and of society at heart. It is the power of parents which they aim to break and they are well on course to do it, by a series of innocuous-sounding administrative changes.

These changes undermine, or forbid, many things which parents profoundly believe are important. The proposition that most parents cannot be trusted with the care and control of their children is both an insult to the vast majority of adults in this country, and a nonsense. If they are untrustworthy in this, with what can they be reasonably trusted? And why should the state know better than its citizens how to bring up children?

The answer to this – that children's rights professionals know better – can be judged in the light of what they have achieved so far. This comes down to only two broad categories, both of which are inimical to what most responsible parents want for their children.

They are: the right for children to behave badly if they want to; and the right to sexual experimentation before they have reached maturity.

Chapter 8

The Swedish Experience

The Nordic Committee for Human Rights is an international non-governmental organisation which aims to increase the rights and freedoms of private individuals and their families against the power of the State. They have opened an Internet web site* collating information about violations of families' rights in Nordic countries.

The nub of their complaint is that children's rights have been used as a vessel for a type of totalitarian interference in the family which is not so different from that previously exercised in the Soviet Union. They point to the fact that there are proportionately between six and twelve times the number of children in care in Sweden as in Japan and more than three times the number in Britain. Of that very large number, a large proportion are taken from their families on the wide grounds given to them by legislation that is designed to prevent 'child-abuse' including of course, smacking.

The lawyers in the NCHR say that they are hampered in collecting precise figures by the fact that all such cases are transferred to the social authorities who keep them 'out of reach' of those wishing to compile statistics. Suffice it to say that according to the evidence of NCHR, many hundreds, if not thousands, of children have been taken from their families and sent far away from ties of kinship, on grounds that would not stand up for a moment outside of Scandinavia. Thousands have been the subject of threatening investigations. Even if parents should win a court order to have their children returned to them, nothing can stop the social services from

*www.nkmr.org

taking their child into immediate care again.

This seemingly wild claim is amply born out by the striking case of the Olsson family which was described in *Readers Digest* in 1991. This ordinary Swedish family took their case to the European Court of Human Rights in 1991 and the facts of this case alone illustrate an abominable state of affairs. Their three children, aged 9, 4 and 22 months were seized from a friend's house by police and social workers because a social worker had made an entirely subjective judgement that the mother could not cope with the children. The children were simply abducted and the parents did not know, *for five months,* where their children had been taken. Eventually, the parents found them living with two separate foster families 600 miles away. The ensuing battle, which took *seven years* to reach the European Court resulted in a decision that the Olsson's rights had been violated and the court awarded them £33,000.

However, the European Court having found that the children had been wrongfully taken did not result in their being returned. The eldest boy of 16 years old was allowed home but the local social services council decided that a move back to their parents would not be in the best interests of the two young children and temporary custody was given to the foster parents. The parents were allowed to see them for just two hours, three times a *year!*

This is not an isolated example as the on-going cases recorded on the web page indicate. One of its contributors is lawyer Liv Westerberg, who has contested many such cases. She says that the distinction between children taken into custody by force and children who have gone into custody with the 'agreement' of their parents, is almost meaningless since parents are rightly intimidated by the power of social workers. 'Sweden,' she says, 'has become a social-welfare prison state'.

This horrible situation suits those who dislike the family for ideological reasons as well as those who simply enjoy power over others. The policy of enforcing adults to be dependent on rights arbitrarily accorded them by the state, says NCHR, has been nurtured and sustained by an extreme form of feminism and a Marxist hatred of the family. 'The feminists shot the patriarch while the socialists took the children'.

It is historically significant that a Swedish organisation known as Save the Children was set up by a group of socialist Swedish women in the early 1920's and its aim was to give the state access to every child born. According to their philosophy, a child was not considered as belonging to the woman, it was always referred to as 'the child' rather than 'her child'. It was the advent of the philosophy of the 'parental state' that found its echo in the statement by Lady Helen Brook, President of the Brook Advisory Centres: 'It is now the privilege of the Parental State to take major decisions – objective unemotional, the State weighs up what is best for the child . . .' [41]

Astrid Lindgren, the famous author, and creator of *Pippi Longstocking,* the poor little girl who was constantly pursued by childcare officers, probably had an intensely personal motive to her writing. She had to leave Sweden in 1926 because she was pregnant and unmarried and, under laws created by the Save the Children organisation a few years earlier, would have had her baby taken from her.

Significantly, the organisation was a major force behind the UN Convention on children's rights and has provided enthusiastic support for the 'child-abuse hysteria' which is currently plaguing Sweden.

And yet in Nordic countries, as everywhere else, children are vastly more at risk of all types of ill-treatment once they are away from their own families. A large study by *Sariola et al* in Finland in 1990 found that sexual abuse of girls at home was less than 0.15%, while the figure for girls living in a non-biological environment was 15 to 30 times higher.

In their muted way, many Swedes are now uneasy about the parlous state of the family in Sweden. Marriage is almost uniquely unpopular amongst them and more than half of all children are born out of wedlock. Those problems which are now becoming familiar to us as being associated with fatherlessness, have produced a generation of children who are doing badly at school and whose bad behaviour renders them unwelcome as visitors to many of their neighbours.

Lawyer and Chief of Police, Soren Alfredsson, drew attention to this fact in an open letter sent to the German Ministry of Justice in December 1992. He was commenting on the proposal to pass the same anti-smacking law in Germany and he begged them, in the light of the terrible Swedish experience, to think again. He said,

> As far as our knowledge goes, judging from the number of indictments and judgements we have in our possession, there have been dozens of cases where normal parents who have tried to curb their children, have been prosecuted, sentenced to prison or fined for child abuse, or have been very close to being prosecuted. The hundreds of thousands of cases which have been reported to the Social Authorities which have given rise to social investigations and dismissed at an early stage are, of course, not included in statistics. Even such cases have damaged both the parents and the children involved."

He goes on to give chapter and verse of 12 cases where parents have been punished by fines, 'summary punishment', losing their job, imprisonment and, in several cases, the removal of their children.

One need not be psychic to perceive that all this interference in family life by the authorities, acts as a potent deterrent to opposition to these laws. Parents are justifiably afraid.

The only people who regularly trumpet what a wonderful place it is for children – though families are never mentioned, – are those activists who would like to see the same sort of scenario developing in Britain.

Those who quote Sweden as a good example of childcare practice should be aware of how secretive the authorities there are about the policies they pursue. This was demonstrated by the revelations in 1998 that the Swedish state had sterilised many thousands of boys and girls for eugenic purposes until well into the 1970s, without the policy becoming known to the public or to those who like to speak of Sweden as Utopia.

Mrs Ruby Harrold-Claesson, Chairman of the Nordic Committee of Human Rights, specifically mentions EPOCH as being a British organisation which disseminates misinformation about Sweden. Her recent paper, *When Parents Become Victims*, details dozens of cases of families smashed by their anti-smacking laws. It is a catch-all device for gaining control over the family rather like the sex-abuse witch-hunt, except much worse. The 120-odd parents, for example, in the Cleveland child-abuse debacle, would not have been able to get their children back if the social workers had been able to say: 'Even if they haven't been sexually abused, they have been smacked'. The majority of parents are sensible mature adults, who would be completely at the mercy of social services personnel.

It is certain that, notwithstanding the soothing assurances of those who advocate a law to make smacking children an offence in Britain, children in Sweden are taken into care by the authorities, and in large numbers. This fact is sufficient to silence any honest admission of parental opinion in the matter. A SIMA poll in Sweden in 1991 found that 35% of women thought smacking children was necessary and another 35% refused to state their position – which speaks for itself.

It is devoutly to be hoped that those people – I believe a

large majority in this country – who do not want to see the parental right to reasonable discipline criminalised, will realise the likely outcome if such a law were to be enacted. It is not an exaggeration to say that it would be the end of the freedom of the family. Henceforward, it would become a state institution with 'caretaker' parents, subservient to social workers and the law, in the most intimate details of family life. Those who do not wish to see this happen should make sure that organisations to which they may belong, do not cast their block vote in support of such a measure.

Conclusion

There have been many tyrannies over time which have attempted to eradicate the family; usually because it gets in the way of a system or ideology. In our own day, the greatest claim to usurp the rights of parents is made by childcare, and other professionals, both medical and legal, who stand to gain by being enabled to take over some of the duties and responsibilities normally undertaken by parents. Their careers, departments and prospects are enlarged by changes which have sent thousands of children into special units in education authorities and social services departments, because normal parental and adult discipline is inhibited or curtailed.

In addition to this easily understood process of colonising the territory normally governed by parents, lies the even less admirable, but still understandable, desire to make money out of young people whom the law has rendered vulnerable to exploitation. There is money to be made out of the sheer inexperience of children and a flourishing condom, counselling and contraceptive industry is already leeching off their vulnerability. You don't need to be psychic to see the benefit to the contraceptive industry of the de-facto abolition of the age of consent for girls, and the proposed dropping of the age of consent for boys will no doubt be catered for contraceptively in the same way.

Some may consider this incredible in view of the findings of Professor Adler of the London Medical School, that HIV infections in 1996 were at their highest ever level amongst young men.[43] It is not disclosed, or perhaps known, whether the 18% increase has anything to do with the lowering of the age of consent from 21 to 18 in 1994 but, in normal circumstances, any such dramatic increase would indicate the need for extreme caution before going any further.

Behind these rather simple, even understandable ambitions, lie forces which are darker and less disclosed, which are antagonistic to the traditional family. In some cases this is for ideological reasons and in others it is because the person, by reason of their chosen life-style, is an outsider to it. Some homosexuals of both sexes want access to children as is plain from their current demand to be allowed to adopt children and to have artificially inseminated children. For them, the natural family is the enemy of all their aspirations and, as some have gone on record saying, its destruction is their principal objective.

The *Gay Liberation Front Manifesto* of 1979 expressed it thus:

> We, along with the women's movement, must fight for something more than reform. We must aim at the abolition of the family so that the sexist, male supremacist system can no longer be nurtured there. The oppression of gay people starts in the most basic unit of society, the family, consisting of the man in charge, a slave as his wife, and their children on whom they force themselves as the ideal models . . . The end of the sexist culture and of the family will benefit all women and gay people.[44]

How all these 'special interest groups', professional, financial and ideological, have found common cause under the umbrella of children's rights, is now a matter of public record. The public, for its part, has been slow to see that what is being done neutralises the power of parents and other responsible adults to protect children and to maintain our culture.

It is not coincidental that the specifically anti-parental ideas enshrined in the philosophy of children's rights should have appeared at this time. For any of the above-mentioned interest groups to succeed in their aims, the power of parents to act for, and protect, their children must be broken, or at least marginalised.

As we have seen, the various movements for children's rights have been either instrumental or decisive in undermining or removing the power of parents and other agencies to protect children by imposing effective discipline upon them. The law itself has been rendered a timid and almost ineffectual tool when it comes to enforcing good behaviour in children and the record levels of delinquency, drug-dependence, sexual disease, illegitimacy and exclusions from school, are living proof of the failure of this essentially ideological and experimental approach.

One would have thought that the time was long overdue when these and other avoidable disasters were simply not considered acceptable any more. Sooner or later there is going to be a backlash, if only because the cost, in human as well as fiscal terms, is too high.

It might help everybody to come to their senses, and look honestly at what is happening, if they realised just how small and unrepresentative are the forces which have master-minded the innovations in the first place. With great skill and guile, they have provided the arguments, briefed the media, and set up the organisations which governments consult when devising their policy. And yet they are a handful of people, when all is said and done.

We should ask ourselves just one question. In the matter of children's rights, is there any area where their influence has been felt, where the result has been good? In schools, children's homes, child-minding groups, foster homes, neighbourhoods or families, the net result of innovations fostered and promoted by children's rights activists has always been the same. Respectable, well qualified people have been driven out by the impossibility of working in an atmosphere where the children can do as they please.

Around 90% of adults questioned replied that they believe chastisement to be necessary as a last resort with naughty children, and so they would be considered ineligible to work in a whole range of places which look after children.

It is no wonder that anxieties are often expressed about the difficulty of recruiting suitable people to work in problem areas and about the poor quality of many applicants, when they have to confine recruitment to that small proportion of the population who agree, both with their working methods and with the results that those methods achieve.

Respectable people who really care about children do not like to see them running amok and getting into more and more trouble without their being able to intervene in any way. They either leave the caring professions or, increasingly, never enter them.

There is an instructive piece on the subject in the professional magazine *Community Care* (October 1997). A senior social services manager had written an earlier piece where he said that he was 'stunned' to find that new social work students had a fear of child protection work and probably would not last in it. A correspondent, obviously in the field himself, replied that the manager "must be the only senior manager in social services who is surprised by the reluctance of newly qualified social workers to enter the child protection field. With the introduction of the climate of fear engendered by the willy-nilly giving of adult rights to children (without children having to accept the equally important responsibilities of adulthood) . . . I am not surprised that there may be a lack of interest. Until social workers are freed from this unbearable weight, I suspect that these quite sensible professionals may well keep looking for quiet little numbers working with elderly people or adults with learning difficulties".

The writer's apprehensions were confirmed in the same

magazine in May 1998 when the Social Work Training Council revealed a "massive decline in the number of applicants for Diploma in Social Work courses" and a corresponding fear about the quality of the profession.

Children's homes today have much the same standing with the public as the Workhouse did in Victorian times. Too many of them are regarded as the road to ruin and this reputation owes a great deal to the fact that they are places where children are allowed to get into trouble through pursuing one or both of the only two 'rights' which really matter to children's rights activists; the right to behave badly and the right to get into premature sexual activity.

Let that be their monument and let history judge whether or not it was an experiment worth making. But for the sake of our children and for sanity in our culture, the rest of us must bestir ourselves to be more vocal in defence of our rights as parents and adults.

We cannot afford, literally or figuratively, to accept meekly the assault on the intelligence and experience of millions of adults in the matter of bringing up our children. Most parents freely chose to have and to raise children and it is a slow, creeping abberation that has allowed anybody else to lay claim to deciding how they should do it. We have laws to protect children against the crimes and excesses of a minority of parents and they should, of course, be vigorously pursued. However, at present, by far the biggest threat to the well-being, good management and happiness of the family, schools and neighbourhoods, is represented by those agencies of the state which have taken it upon themselves to dictate how children should be managed.

As long ago as August 1994 Alastair Palmer wrote in the *Spectator* about the methods used by Surrey Social Services departments against parents they believed, on the slimmest and most unlikely evidence, to be a danger to their child. A front door was broken down by eight baton-wielding men wearing balaclavas and helmets. They turned out to be policemen, accompanied by social workers and they were acting on an accusation made in Holland about the husband who was the father of a six week old baby. He was thrown to the floor, sustaining a cut to his face that required eight stitches, whilst a policeman stood with a foot on his neck. His child was seized and carried off together with his wife. He was separated from his wife and child for three weeks, his civil rights completely abrogated, on the say-so of officials investigating possible child abuse.

As Palmer said, the scene was more reminiscent of Nuremburg in 1936 than Surrey in 1994:

> Arbitrary and tyrannical uses of state powers are tolerated in child-abuse investigations by local council, by lawyers, by judges, and ultimately by ministers which would create uproar if anything similar occurred even in the course of an investigation into the most hideous terrorist bombing"

He went on to say that if it were an isolated incident, it could perhaps be discounted or ignored, but that there is evidence that the injustice meted out to this couple and their baby is happening to hundreds of people throughout the country:

> The rush to judgement, presumption of guilt, crass and insensitive treatment of both parents and infants, and utter indifference to the trauma their action may cause – all of which the 1989 Children Act was designed to prevent – still seem characteristic of the way that social services departments all over the country deal with cases of this kind.

It is the 'utter indifference' of the children's rights people to these cases that is so shocking and so revealing. Shocking because they are the only people who are organised, who receive regular attention from the media when they speak, and who receive millions of pounds to represent the rights of children; and they remain indifferent to this kind of thing happening up and down the country. Nor do they publicise it or provide some sort of repository where complaints, and an account of their treatment can be recorded by the victims.

It is revealing because it demonstrates, far more clearly than their words can, that children's rights organisations do not regard parents and children as part of a unit. The family and its well-being, is not their concern, and their well-known, exceedingly well-financed organisations have a narrow focus that completely ignores the widespread abuse of children, via the persecution of their families.

Individuals and families can be targeted and picked-off singly by bullying bureaucrats who enjoy immunity for what they do. It is an offence for anyone who is not a public official to expose any aspect of a public official's response to an allegation of child abuse, and even to name any of the officials in a case. They are free to behave in the same way over and over again and, as Alasdair Palmer said, this law protects both tyrannical and incompetent officials. They can bulldoze their way through the guidelines of the Children Act not only without penalty but without even being found out.

Lest anyone should think that this is a typically right-wing perspective, let the last word go to that stalwart of the Left, Ken Livingstone. Commenting on a similar case in his own constituency, where a family was terrorised, ruined and broken by mindless accusations against a father that were later dropped, without redress or even an apology, he said, 'I always tell people who complain to Brent Council to imagine they are dealing with a cross between a used-car salesman and a Nazi war criminal. They systematically lie in virtually every department, virtually all the time'.

One would think, that those who helped form the Children Act and who constantly invoke its ideals, would have some mechanism for investigating its abuses? If they are unaware of them then it shows just how indifferent they really are to the subject that has been the means of providing them with gainful employment over the years.

No doubt one of the reasons why they just don't want to know about these things, is that they are seeking to include smacking children in the canon of 'child abuse'. Then we can expect similar measures to be taken in cases where a parent is suspected of having laid a corrective hand on a child. Indeed, it has already happened as in the case of the Staffordshire teacher who slapped his son, was arrested and imprisoned for fifteen hours before being released - but excluded from his home for nearly three months.[45]

I only hope those organisations who have blithely signed up their membership in support of EPOCH's campaign to get smacking children subject to legal sanction, realise what they are doing and what it will mean. It will certainly mean, as it has in Sweden, that hundreds of families will be persecuted and broken on the say-so of state officials acting on instructions to enforce the law against parental discipline.

The hold they and their ideas have on our culture must be broken and the first step towards that goal is to recognise who they are, and how few. After all, there is no end to the power they could seek in the end. The state already thinks it has the right to prescribe bedtimes, how much homework is done, the type of sexual perversion children should be instructed in and whether the child should be engaging in sexual activity or not. For the first time in our history they have begun to talk about 'curfews' to curb bad behaviour and even imposing restrictive or financial penalties on adults for being unable to control children.

In Paul Boateng we had a junior Health Minister who was more than usually down to earth; but he, like so many of his predecessors, may be intimidated by the misleading claims of 'massive support' for more state power to control parents. He would do far better to cast an honest and appraising eye on what their advice has led to so far and to listen to that majority of the public who would see him as a hero and a saviour if he were to set about curbing the 'rights' that have been somehow acquired by overweening officials to the detriment of ordinary civil rights.

'Listening to the People' was prime minister Tony Blair's promise for 1997, and it proved popular. There is an urgent need to consider this promise honestly today, and not connive at the subjugation of the populace by tiny, unrepresentative pressure groups who have already done so much to disrupt families, schools and communities. The return of common sense and good order in family and community affairs is something that could re-moralise society and counter the current malaise.

The assertion of children's rights in their current form is both bogus and inconsistent. They do not, for example, propose to raise children to the level of adults where they would be named, prosecuted and punished for violence and disorderly behaviour. Neither are they proposing that children be allowed to choose if they drink, smoke or attend school. The 'rights' which they are prepared to support conform to a strict agenda and do not include such things. In other words, we are not talking about genuine children's rights at all. We are talking about the right of some adults – and certainly not ordinary parents – to decide what children shall and shall not be allowed to do. Children themselves are just the means by which they achieve their aims. Their effect, if not intentions, is to reduce us all to the level of dependent children, waiting to be told by Nanny State what rights we have left with which to control our own lives and to make decisions for the welfare of our families.

In fact, this new *de facto* authoritarianism was beautifully analyzed by James Heartfield in an article where he pointed out that the extension of children's rights was not an increase of liberty, but a degradation of the meaning of individual rights:

> A child is competent before the law to the extent that an array of lawyers, social workers and judges exercise his rights on his behalf. If these are the sorts of rights that the rest of us should expect, then we had better get used to being treated like children.

> Most insidiously of all, 'empowering' children is the means by which the state disguises its domination as liberation. If the argument for the curtailment of adults' rights were put without the justification of recognising children's rights, it would read 'We, the state, demand the right to decide how you, incompetents, live your lives'. Few people would accept such a proposition. But put in terms of children's rights, it begins to assume the character of a reasonable idea.[46]

Quite so! And isn't it lucky that all those pressure groups, with an axe to grind or something to gain, shuffled forward at just the right time to make the claim in the name of children and on behalf of authoritarianism? Never at the cutting edge of intellectual analysis, many of those involved in charities and other well-meaning organisations, as well as those prompted by less altruistic motives, have lent their weight to measures which, in the name of the rights of the child, have done untold harm to an immense number of people. They have helped to put a hammer in the hand of government officials which could, if we are not more alert to the danger, smash our liberties in the future in much the same way as they have already smashed the lives of so many individuals and the happiness and well-being of so many families.*

If the price of freedom is eternal vigilance then we need to pay much more attention to what is being done to our liberties in the name of children's rights. They are a wolf in sheep's clothing at present, devouring our liberties in the name of children who, for the most part neither need, nor want, nor benefit from their attention.

The reputation of social workers has been fatally compromised in the matter of child protection as a result of excesses perpetrated by some officials, which reverberate around a community like a gun-shot. As a result, many parents must be able to frighten children merely by mentioning that they will be called in, which rather defeats the purpose of their existence in the first place.

There is always a risk attached to freedom and family freedoms are no different. We have never been as subject to the dictats of an empowered class of officials as we are now, hamstrung and harried in the name of our own children's rights. It is high time we got back some of the autonomy we have lost to them so that we may do a better job than they have done in the last few disastrous years.

* Parents who are being coerced by social services personnel should seek advice from Child Rescue. Its director, Gerry Howard, helps more than a hundred families a week from his Brighton Office. Other branches are now operational and they aim to open a web page where parents will be able to share information and their experience of bureaucratic bullying and what to do about it. Telephone number 01273 692947.

References

References

1. UN Convention on the Rights of the Child, 1989, Preamble, paragraphs 5 and 6

2. *Building Small Democracies,* Children's Rights Office, funded by Calouste Gulbenkian Foundation, June 1995, p.12

3. Gerison Lansdown, *Taking Part: Children's participation in decision making,* Institute for Public Policy Research, June 1995, pp.34-35

4. Lord Mackay. Introducing the Children Bill for its second reading *(Hansard,* 6 December 1988, col.490) and quoted in *Children's Legal Centre briefing on the Children Act*

5. Gerison Lansdown, *Taking Part: Children's participation in decision making,* Institute for Public Policy Research, June 1995, p.7

6. *Ibid,* p.8

7. *Childright,* magazine of the Children's Legal Centre, November 1985

8. Nicola Wells, 'Who *really* wants a law against smacking?' *Families for Discipline,* Issue 5, Spring 1997

9. 'The Truth about the NCMA Vote', *Families for Discipline,* Issue 2, Summer 1994

10. Anne Davis, *Confident Parenting,* Souvenir Press, 1997, pp. 54, 55

11. 'A New Epoch for Families?' *Families for Discipline,* Issue 1, Autumn 1993

12. Nicola Wells, *op cit*

13. *The Psychologist,* September 1993

14. Nicola Wells, *op cit*

15. Working Towards a Children's Rights Commissioner, *Annual Report of the Children's Rights Office,* p.1

16. *Learning to Live with Sex* for 13- 16 year olds, Family Planning Association, 1974

17. Calder & Boyars, *Boy Girl Man Woman,* London 1971,

18. Paedophile Action for Liberation, 1976

19. Michael Schofield, Promiscuity, 1975

20. Michael Schofield, *Age of Consent;* paper on Sexual Offences, evidence to the Criminal Law Revision Committee, NCCL, 1976.

21. James le Fanue, *The Daily Telegraph,* 11.3.97

22. *Ibid,* 21.6.96

23. *Ibid.*

24. *Magpie,* Issue 10, 1977

25. *Pink Triangles,* Alyson Publications, Boston, 1980, p.91

26. Letter to executive committee of PIE, 19.4.83

27. Mike McNair & Jamie Gough, *Gay Liberation in the Eighties,* Pluto Press Ltd, London, 1985

28. *The Mail on Sunday,* 24.11.96

29. 'Demons of the Dark', *The Guardian,* 12.6.96

30. *The Daily Telegraph,* 8.3.97

31. *The Daily Telegraph,* 24.5.95

32. *Child Molestation and Homosexuality,* Family Research Institute, 1993.

33. K Freud, R I Watson, 'The proportion of heterosexual and homosexual paedophiles amongst sex offenders against children', *Journal of Sexual and Marital Therapy,* 1992, 18 pp.34-43

34. *The Times*, 18.7.90

35. *The Guardian,* 5.4.97

36. *Taking Children Seriously*, Calouste Gulbenkian Foundation, 1991

37. Interview; CRO Director with a reseacher, 1996

38. Gillian Schofield and June Thoburn, *Child Protection: the voice of the child in decision-making,* Institute for Public Policy Research, 1996

39. *The Daily Telegraph*, 12.10.98

40. Gerison Lansdown, *Taking Part: Children's participation in decision making,* Institute for Public Policy Research, June 1995, p.40

41. Letter *The Times*, 16.2.80

42. *The Times,* 12.3.90

43. *British Medical Journal*, 14.6.97

44. *Gay Liberation Front Manifesto,* London, 1971, rev. 1979, pp. 1, 7, 8, 12

45. *Daily Mail*, 5.9.96

46. James Heartfield, *Living Marxism*, October 1993

Recommended Reading

ALL MUST HAVE PRIZES by Melanie Phillips

The author charts the 'de-education of Britain' which has been taking place over the past thirty years or so, resulting in a rising tide of illiteracy and ignorance, the undermining of the family and the moral codes essential for a civilised society. Yet many educationalists, hidebound by the out-moded tenets of moral relativism, still appear unable to accept the evidence so clearly presented in this remarkable book.

Little, Brown & Co   384pp   Price: **£9.99**

BROKEN HOMES & BATTERED CHILDREN
by Robert Whelan

While there has been a high level of concern at public and governmental level about the apparent increase in child abuse, very little research has been carried out into the relationship between the type of household children live in and their risk of being abused. That research has now been carried out. The findings show the correlation between incomplete or broken families and child abuse.

Family Education Trust   96pp (A4)   Price: **£5.00**

CHARACTER BUILDING:
a guide for parents and teachers   by David Isaacs

The author, a distinguished educationalist, offers ideas and suggestions on how parents and teachers can help the all-round development of children. Approached from the viewpoint of moral habits, emphasis is on character building. Taking 24 virtues Professor Isaacs shows how the child - at different ages - can be encouraged to be obedient, industrious, generous, sincere, optimistic, prudent and sociable, and so on.

Four Courts Press   262pp   Price: **£7.50**

CHARLES MURRAY AND THE UNDERCLASS
by Charles Murray

This book includes Murray's earlier works, The Emerging British Underclass and Underclass: the Crisis Deepens. His thesis, that the underclass represents a type of poverty characterised by deviant attitudes towards parenting, work and crime, has been controversial. It is also difficult to resist as the social fabric obviously deteriorates.

Institute of Economic Affairs   180pp   Price: **£6.00**

FAMILIES WITHOUT FATHERHOOD
by Norman Dennis and George Erdos

Following an introduction by Professor A H Halsey, the very doyen of ethical socialism, the authors survey the enormous volume of statistical evidence which shows that children from uncommitted parents do very much worse by every indicator. They condemn attempts by 'experts' to dismiss the obvious link between outbreaks of inner-city rioting and family breakdown by blaming unemployment and poverty.

Institute of Economic Affairs   132pp   Price: **£3.50**

FAREWELL TO THE FAMILY ? by Patricia Morgan

Profound social and economic consequences of a revolution towards reproductive behaviour has detached childbearing from the commitment of parents within marriage. The rearing of children has become increasingly the responsibility of the state. These trends are not accidental, but the result of policies pursued by governments, often at the instigation of lobby groups.

Institute of Economic Affairs   200pp   Price: **£5.00**

MAKING FAMILIES WORK by Margaret Grimer

A response to the International Year of the Family, the author illustrates the growth and progression of critical situations. It covers all stages of family life and changes that have to be confronted. A positive and encouraging book, written with warmth.

Cassell   122pp   Price: **£9.99**

THE HIDDEN COSTS OF CHILDCARE by Patricia Morgan

Comprehensive childcare to enable mothers to join the labour force has become widely accepted. The author has examined and analysed research material from the UK and overseas suggesting that childcare at an early age may have deleterious effects on many aspects of child development. The hidden costs are the costs to the child and to society itself: childcare children evince problems with concentration, language, underachievement, and attachment with peers and parents.

Family Education Trust   56pp   Price: **£2.00**

THE NECESSARY FAMILY and how to support it
by Hugo de Burgh and Robert Whelan

Married parents living together is *the necessary family*. To found a family now is, for many, to opt for a life of disadvantage and deprivation. The authors suggest how changes to the fiscal system can remedy the situation, and re-affirm the status of marriage. This important and timely report should be read by policy makers of all political persuasions, and by married couples themselves.

Family Education Trust   64pp   Price: **£4.00**

RISING CRIME AND THE DISMEMBERED FAMILY
by Norman Dennis

The author calls attention to the role of a new class of 'conformist intellectuals' in undermining what common sense tells us about rising crime and family breakdown. They deny that the family is breaking down. It is only changing, they say. Nor, in their view, has there been a rise in crime, only an increase in 'moral panic'. Norman Dennis demolishes these claims by carefully drawing attention to the facts.

Institute of Economic Affairs   93pp   Price: **£3.00**

SEX AND SOCIAL ENGINEERING by Valerie Riches

The author reveals the historical background, motivations and social consequences of the movement to give children value-free instruction for sexual activity. She details the highly organised international network and connections between the sex education lobby and the population control movement.

Family Education Trust   28pp   Price: **£1.50**

THE SEXUAL DEAD-END by Stephen Green

This important book represents the culmination of seven years of research into the homosexual network. It is an invaluable guide to the progress of the 'gay rights' movement, its current agenda, and its effect upon the family and society. The author demonstrates how the paedophiles, realising that their demands for access to children were unacceptable, made their cause respectable by adopting the language of civil rights.

Broad View   482pp   Price: **£8.00**

WHO CARES FOR CHILDREN ? by Valerie Riches

A court action in the 80s sought assurance that children under the age of consent would not be prescribed contraception or abortion without the knowledge and consent of parents. The Law Lords ruled against parents. The case provoked unprecedented debate on the responsibilities and rights of parents.

Who Cares for Children? argues that the significance of the case lay in the relationship revealed between families and government. Who is responsible for the upbringing of children: their parents, or the state?

Family Education Trust   32pp   Price: **£1.50**

WHO NEEDS PARENTS? by Patricia Morgan

This is a remarkable critique of the relentless propaganda surrounding the promotion of childcare. Patricia Morgan argues that the debate is charged with ideology without knowledge of the academic research. This book is important reading for those concerned about the effects of childcare and early education in Britain and the USA.

Institute of Economic Affairs   165pp   Price: **£5.00**

Appendices

Appendix A

Organisations, Commissions, Working Groups and Companies and the involvement of key people in the promotion of children's rights ideology.

	FLFS	CLC	ACE	STOPP	CSIE	EPOCH	APP'CH
John Pinkerton							
Christine Walby							
Catriona Williams							
Gerison Lansdown							
Rachel Hodgkin		☐				☐	☐
Philippa Russell					☐		
Martin Rosenbaum		☐	☐	☐		☐	☐
Zarrina Kurtz		☐					
Nicholas Peacey	☐					☐	☐
Peter Newell	■	■	■	■	■	■	■
Nicholas Doyle	☐		☐				
Kathleen Marshall							
John Tomlinson		☐					
Mark Vaughan					☐		
Penelope Leach						☐	☐
Allan Levy							
Paul Curno							
Anne Weyman							
Robert Smith							

A   THE ORGANISATIONS

FLFS   First London Free School Ltd. Est. 1972 dissolved 1992. Part funding from Calouste Gulbenkian Foundation.

CLC   Children's Legal Centre. Est. 1979. Part funding from Calouste Gulbenkian Foundation.

ACE   Advisory Centre for Education. Educational rights organisation. Part funding from Calouste Gulbenkian Foundation.

STOPP   Society of Teachers Opposed to Physical Punishment. Dissolved 1989 post Children's Act 1989. Funds transferred to EPOCH.

CSIE   Centre for Studies on Inclusive Education Ltd. Est. 1987. To advance education and training of children and young people with special education needs. Funding from the Calouste Gulbenkian Foundation.

EPOCH   End Physical Punishment of Children. Est. 1986 and linked directly to APPROACH (Association for the Protection of All Children) by membership and directorships. Funded by Calouste Gulbenkian Foundation.

APPROACH   Association for the Protection Of All Children. Est. 1989 with funds from STOPP and Calouste Gulbenkian Foundation.

IPSEA   Independent Panel for Special Education Advice Ltd. Est. 1987. Providing independent advice and expert second opinion for parents of children who come within the scope of the 1981 Education Act.

CG1993   Calouste Gulbenkian Foundation published and funded a report "One scandal too many" - a case for comprehensive protection of children in all settings.

	IPSEA	CG1993	CG1995	CRDU	CRO	CG1991	CG1996
John Pinkerton				■	■		■
Christine Walby				■	■		
Catriona Williams				■	■		■
Gerison Lansdown				■	■		■
Rachel Hodgkin		■	■	■	■	■	■
Philippa Russell	■	■	■				
Martin Rosenbaum						■	■
Zarrina Kurtz	■						
Nicholas Peacey							
Peter Newell	■	■	■	■	■	■	■
Nicholas Doyle	■						
Kathleen Marshall		■	■	■	■		■
John Tomlinson		■					
Mark Vaughan	■						
Penelope Leach			■			■	■
Allan Levy		■	■				■
Paul Curno		■	■	■	■	■	■
Anne Weyman				■	■		
Robert Smith				■	■		■

Co-ordinated by Peter Newell, the relevant members, advisors and contributors to the report are listed under CG1.

CG1995 Calouste Gulbenkian Foundation commissioned a report "Children and Violence" - a case for the conclusion that the roots of violence go back to childhood and are buried in the family. Co-ordinated by Peter Newell, the relevant members and advisors to the commission are listed under CG2.

CRDU Children's Rights Development Unit Ltd. Est. 1992. To promote the implementation of the UN Convention on the Rights of the Child. Part funding from Calouste Gulbenkian Foundation.

CRO Children's Rights Office. Projection of the CRDU to develop strategies for the implementation of the office of a Children's Rights Commissioner. Part funding from Calouste Gulbenkian Foundation.

CG1991 Calouste Gulbenkian Foundation published and funded a report "Taking Children Seriously" - a proposal for the establishment of a Children's Rights Commissioner. The relevant members of the advisory group are listed under CG3.

CG1996 Calouste Gulbenkian Foundation published and funded a report "Effective Government Structures for Children" - a proposal for ensuring that central government is responsive to the needs and rights of children. Co-ordinated by Peter Newell and Rachel Hodgkin. The relevant members, advisors and contributors to the commission are listed under CG4. This report continued the strategies of the 1991 proposals for a Children's Rights Commissioner funded by the Calouste Gulbenkian Foundation and prepared under the auspices of APPROACH.

Appendix B

The people and their Connections with the organisations in which they are involved and their functions in those organisations.

B   CONNECTIONS

Peter Newell

Ex Director	First London Free School Ltd	**FLFS**
Ex Education Officer	National Council for Civil Liberties	NCCL
Ex Company Sec.	Advisory Centre for Education	**ACE**
Founder Director	Children's Legal Centre	**CLC**
Treasurer	Society of Teachers Opposed to Physical Punishment	**STOPP**
Founder	Association for Protection of All Children	**APPROACH**
Founder	End Physical Punishment of Children	**EPOCH**
Founder/Director	Centre for Studies on Inclusive Education	**CSIE**
Founder/Director	Independent Panel for Special Education Advice	**IPSEA**
Chairman	Children's Rights Office	**CRO**
Chairman	Children's Rights Development Unit	**CRDU**
Coordinator	Cal. Gulbenkian : "One Scandal too Many" 1993	**CG1**
Coordinator	Cal. Gulbenkian : "Children and Violence" 1995	**CG2**
Coordinator	Cal. Gulbenkian : "Taking Children Seriously" 1991	**CG3**
Coordinator	Cal. Gulbenkian : "Effective Govt. Structures 1996	**CG4**

Gerison Lansdown

Staff Director	**CRO**
Director	**CRDU**
Ex Director	Child Poverty Action Group CPAG
Ex Director	CPAG Limited
Advisor	**CG4**
Member	National Forum (SCAA) on Educ. & Community Values

Robert Smith

Ex Treasurer	**CRO**
Ex Director	**CRDU**
Advisor	**CG4**
Director	UNICEF - UK

Paul Curno

Social Work Trainer	National Youth Bureau NYB
Dep. Director	Calouste Gulbenkian UK (Funding) **CG**

Ex Director	**CRDU**
Ex Comp. Secretary	**CRO**
Member	**CG1**
Advisor	**CG2**
Member	**CG3**
Member	**CG4**

Catriona Williams

Director	**CRDU**
Member	**CRO**
Director Children in Wales	CIW
Advisor	**CG4**
Chairman European Forum for Child Welfare (UK)	

Kathleen Marshall

Member	**CRO**
Director	**CRDU**
Member	**CG1**
Member	**CG2**
Advisor	**CG4**
Director Scottish Child Law Centre	SCLC

Rachel Hodgkin

Member	CRO
Director	CRDU
Founder	APPROACH
Founder	EPOCH
Ex Director	CLC
Member	CG1
Member	CG2
Member	CG3
Coordinator	CG4
Prin. Policy Off. National Children's Bureau	NCB
Ex Director Advice Advocacy & Representation Service for Children	AARSC
Executive	UNICEF - UK

Christine Walby

Member	CRO
Director	CRDU
Director	NCB

Anne Weyman

Member	CRO
Director	CRDU
Ex Director	Brook Advisory Centres Ltd BAC
Director	NCB

Allan Levy QC

Legal Advisor	NCB
Advisor	CG1
Member	CG2
Advisor	CG4

John Pinkerton

Director	CRDU
Director	CRO
Contributor	CG4

Zarrina Kurtz

Advisor	NCB
Ex Director	CLC
Member	CG1

Nicholas Peacey

Founder Director	FLFS
Member	APPROACH
Member	EPOCH

Philippa Russell

Director	CSIE
Director	IPSEA
Member	CG1
Member	CG2

Martin Rosenbaum

Staff	CLC
Coordinator	STOPP
Ex Director	ACE
Member	APPROACH
Member	EPOCH
Coordinator	CG3
Contributor	CG4

Penelope Leach

Member	APPROACH
Member	EPOCH
Advisor	CG2
Member	CG3
Member	CG4

Nicholas Doyle

Ex Director	ACE
Director	IPSEA
Founder Director	FLFS

Mark Vaughan

Director	IPSEA
Ex Director	CSIE

John Tomlinson

Director	NCB
Advisor	CG1
Director	ACE